Learning to
LOVE

Learning to

LOVE

by Willard Tate

Introduction by
Zig Ziglar

LEARNING TO LOVE

Copyright © 1988 by Gospel Advocate Co.

Published by Christian Communications
A division of the Gospel Advocate Co.
P.O. Box 150, Nashville, TN 37202
ISBN 0-89225-321-5
Second Printing, September 1988

Dedication

This book is dedicated to Bobbie, my companion, who has stood with me all these years. Without her strength and help, this book could have never come together. She has been a wonderful mother to our children, a devoted Christian, a wonderful, faithful and loving partner and super grandmother. Thanks for teaching me to love.

Introduction

In his book, *Learning to Love*, my friend Willard Tate draws on his years of experience as a university professor, basketball coach, and motivational speaker, to show us the importance of developing right relationships with others and with God.

He shows us how to break out of our comfort zones and to successfully experience the joy of right relationships.

This book gives us the confidence to be somebody, not necessarily in the way the world views it, but from God's viewpoint. It helps us remember that our only meaningful self-worth is a gift from God.

Willard gives us a perspective of what happens when we learn to believe in ourselves, not because of what we are worth, but because of what Christ in us is worth. It can turn our lives around through the power of forgiveness freeing us for dynamic living.

I appreciate the practical tips on how to put others first, and how we can learn the joy of serving others.

This book will help you become people builders and you will learn to communicate from your heart.

Zig Ziglar

Contents

PART 1

Developing the Capacity to Love

Chapter 1

Learning to Love

A few years ago, I was relaxing in my backyard one night, enjoying a big, beautiful Texas sunset. As I sat there and took it all in, I did a little daydreaming, or what I like to call visualizing. I imagined that I was an old man coming to the end of my life, and a television reporter had come to interview me. "Mr. Tate," he said, "you've spoken all around the country and given people a lot of advice. At this point in your life, if you had just *one thing* you could pass on to the next generation, what would it be?"

I remember that in my mind's eye I took the microphone without a moment's hesitation and answered, "They should know that the key to life is the ability to establish and maintain long-lasting relationships." Long-lasting relationships—with God, with family and friends, and even a good relationship with yourself—that's really what life's all about, isn't it? The key to life certainly *isn't* in what you own, and it's not even in what you've done. It's in the lives that have touched you and that you've influenced. Since I did that bit of visualizing, I've become more convinced than ever that the answer I gave that imaginary reporter was the right one.

We all want strong, intimate, long-lasting relationships, don't we? They're what make life worth living. Looking at it from the negative side, there's probably no greater desperation in the world than the feeling of utter loneliness that comes to those who don't have *any* such relationships.

So how do we build this kind of relationship, and how do we keep them strong once they're formed? The answer to both questions is wrapped up in one little word, *love*. Now, although that word is little, there's nothing simple about it. It's not just a warm, fuzzy feeling. It's much more. Not only that, but it's also something that doesn't come naturally to us. Our natural tendency is to be selfish, to seek our *own* pleasure and fulfillment. But when you love someone, you put *his* interests above your own.

Another important thing we have to realize about love is that it's not something we automatically know how to do. Imagine putting someone who's never been in an airplane inside the cockpit of a big 747 jumbo jet and telling him he's supposed to fire up the engines and fly the plane from Dallas to Tokyo. That wouldn't make much sense, would it—it would be downright ridiculous and dangerous. Well, human emotions and relationships are much more complex than the controls of any jetliner, so it should be no surprise that we can't just "wing it" when it comes to relationships.

On a recent flight to Albuquerque, there was a delay for some equipment repair. In an effort to ease the stress of the passengers, the pilot became quite chatty. He even invited us up to the cockpit to look around, and the little boy in me responded. While there, I related what I say in my seminars about marriage versus piloting. They agreed that it was certainly right, for the airplane was *predictable*. You must have to learn it, then it's simple for it does the same thing *every time* (Of course, they weren't saying that all other conditions, i.e., weather, birds, etc., were always the same!). But *people* are not predictable; mates are neither simple or predictable. We need some training!

But here's the good news. Even though love doesn't come naturally to us, and even though we don't instinctively know how to love in a way that builds the kinds of relationships we want, *we can learn to love the way we should, the way we all want to*. Through the Bible and lessons God teaches by often-painful experience, I trust God Himself will teach us what we need to know, and then He'll give us the strength to put that love into life-changing action. "And hope does not disappoint us, because God has poured out his love into our hearts by the Holy Spirit, whom he has given us" (Rom. 5:5). That's the purpose of this book.

Now, before we can give love to others, we need to feel loved and feel good about ourselves. That's not a selfish attitude; it's just a recognition of the way we're made. You can't draw water from an empty well, and we can't give to others what we don't have ourselves. Thus, in the first part of the book, we'll look at how we can develop a healthy sense of self-esteem regardless of how poorly we may think of ourselves now and in spite of the way the world system works to tear down our self-esteem. It begins with an appreciation of how and how much God loves us, and it proceeds through what we say to ourselves, our self-talk, and our willingness to make positive changes in our lives, even though any kind of change makes us uncomfortable at first.

Then, in the second part of the book, we'll learn how we can love others and build the kind of relationships with them that we all want, those long-lasting bonds that make life meaningful and worth living. We'll explore practical ways to help people feel accepted, for-given, valuable, and loved.

In the subject we'll take up next, you'll learn how painful it is to make *any* kind of change.

Chapter 2

The Need for Change

One time I was speaking in a seminar, and at the break a man came up to me. He was as serious as he could be, and his face had turned just about sheet white. He said, "I don't know about all that stuff you're saying about being motivated by love. I'd be afraid to give up fear." He was saying that he recognized he was motivated in his life by fear, and that as bad as that might be, if he gave it up, he wouldn't have anything left to motivate him. But he had obviously never felt real, unconditional love or he wouldn't have said that.

"Don't be afraid to give up fear."

Still, when we talk about learning to love God, ourselves, and others, we need to understand that it means some things are going to have to change. Change is an unavoidable part of life, and we'll never grow in anything if we don't change.

My guess is that if I were to ask whether you'd like to see some changes in your life, you would answer yes without hesitation. We all know there are things in our lives that could be better, relationships that aren't what we'd like. There's room for improvement. So we recognize the need for change. Naturally, we hope the changes in our lives will be changes from bad to good, from good to better, or even from better to best.

But I've got some bad news for you. We may want to see positive changes in our lives, but the fact is that things, including relationships, tend *not* to change. They stay basically the same from one day to the next. The tide goes out and comes back in again. The sun rises, and the sun sets. If a guy came up to me at the end of a day and said, "What's happening? Why is it getting dark?" I'd say, "You haven't been around long, have you? It does that nearly every day." In the same way, the seasons follow one another reliably year after year—winter, spring, summer, and fall.

When it comes to relationships, the news is even more discouraging. They're more likely to change than the sun and the seasons, but the problem is that left to themselves, *they usually get worse, not better.* You can compare relationships to gardens. I know a little about gardening, and I know that unless a garden is tended regularly and carefully, the weeds will soon take over. You don't even have to plant them. They just grow up automatically.

In the same way, we have to weed every relationship—our marriage, our friendships, our church family—or troubles will spring up automatically and soon take over.

"All you have to do to lose is do nothing."

You know, it's not even necessary to do *wrong* things for relationships to go downhill. Just do nothing. It's

kind of like being a salmon that has to struggle up-
stream to get where it needs to go. If the fish stops
swimming and drifts with the stream, it'll soon be
heading in the wrong direction. Likewise if we just
drift along in our relationships, we'll go the wrong
way.

A wise man once said that all that's necessary for the
triumph of evil is for good people to do nothing. And
while he was speaking primarily about society as a
whole and about governments, the same thing is true
on the level of personal relationships.

When I was a young person just out of high school, I
thought there was a corner somewhere, and if I could
stand on that corner and be dressed just right, before
long a train would come along and take me off to
Never Never Land, where I'd live happily ever after. In
my youthful ignorance, I didn't know there wasn't any
such train, or that even if there were it would be going
in the wrong direction.

How We Change Things

So how *do* relationships change for the better? Very
simple. They'll get better when *we* change for the better. Most of the time we sit around and wait for that
other person to change. We say to ourselves, "I'll
change when I finally see that he's willing to change
first." And you know what's happening, don't you?
He's sitting in his easy chair saying the same thing
about us! As long as we're all thinking that way,
nothing will ever change. Someone has to take the initiative and be the first to change for the better. And if
we really want our relationships to improve, that someone should be us.

Do you want a better husband? Then become a better wife. Do you want better leadership in your

church? Then become a better member. Do you want a better boss in your work? Then become a better employee. If you're the boss, do you want better workers? Then become a better boss. The fact is that almost always, when we get better, the people we come in contact with get better in response.

---

*"If you keep on doing
what you've always been doing,
you're going to keep on getting
what you've always been getting."*

Can I guarantee that will *always* happen? Can I promise that if you become a better husband or wife, your spouse will also get better? No, I can't offer such a guarantee. It doesn't always work out that way, though most of the time it does. But here's what I *can* promise: If you keep on doing the same things that have made any given relationship what it is today, you're going to get the same results you always have. There's no way things are going to get any better.

---

*"Things get better
when I get better."*

The Pain of Change

Now, let's say you agree with what I've said so far and you're willing to work at changing yourself in the hope that not only will you improve, but so also will your relationships. As soon as you actually begin to change, you'll encounter another difficult reality of life. You'll find that there's a natural resistance to change because it forces us out of our comfort zones.

All of us, whether our situations and relationships are basically good or bad, have reached compromises and accommodations with our circumstances and have some sort of "normal" life. Now, normal for one person may be very different from someone else's normal, but we each have our routines and standard ways of relating, and there's some comfort in knowing what to expect from day to day. We like to be in familiar places and circumstances most of the time—again, even if what's familiar for us is far from ideal in someone else's eyes, or even in our own eyes if we're able to be objective about it. The man I mentioned at the beginning of this chapter is a perfect example of this. And those routines, those standard ways of relating, and those familiar circumstances make up our comfort zones.

Once we start to change, even if it's for the better, we begin to leave those comfort zones. We move away from the familiar and into a frightening world where we don't know quite what to expect anymore. Ouch! Our natural tendency will be to withdraw immediately back into the routines we know from the past. This is when the determination to change for the better is really put to the test. It isn't easy to pass that test, but knowing ahead of time what's going to happen should help us stand firm and then move ahead in the direction we want to go.

If you're not sure what I mean when I talk about comfort zones, try a little experiment. If you attend church regularly, you probably sit in the same place almost every Sunday—right side or left, front or back. So the next time you go, make a point of sitting somewhere other than your usual spot. If you like to sit on the left in the back, go to the right side up front. You'll be amazed how uncomfortable this little change makes you feel. If you're a man, you probably shave the parts of your face in a certain order every morning. Tomorrow, try doing it in reverse order. Again, this small shift in your routine will make you feel terribly awkward.

"If I ever grow
I must choose to hurt."

The challenge of leaving our comfort zones points out another important fact about change: We know going in that it's going to hurt, which means that *a decision to grow and change must be a deliberate, willful choice to suffer.* That's really tough. No one in his right mind likes pain. Yet the only way we'll ever satisfy our longing to be better, to become more Christlike, to grow more mature, to improve our relationships by first improving ourselves, is to step out of those comfort zones and accept the hurt that's sure to come. That's not easy for me to say, and it's even harder for us to do, but there's no other way.

A Call to Submission

When all is said and done, the need for us to change and the willingness to hurt that it requires of us boil down to one crucial thing—a call to humble submission to the lordship of Jesus Christ. As I said before, we want the other person to change first. That's because of our pride. We also stubbornly resist change because we want to stay in control of our lives, and we don't want to suffer the loss of our comfort zones. But that's not what God has in mind for us. The apostle Paul wrote in Romans 12:2, "Do not conform any longer to the pattern of this world, but be transformed by the renewing of your mind."

God's will for us is that we change continually for the better, always growing more like His Son and our Savior, the Lord Jesus. That's what it means to be His follower, His disciple. More than any other reason, this is why we must accept the challenge to change, even though it will surely bring us pain. Sad to say, *most people will never make that choice.* But if you do, one of the things you will learn is how to love like your heavenly Father.

Feeling Like a Hypocrite

In my seminars I often ask people, "How many of you like phonies? Raise your hand." No one raises a hand. Then I ask, "How many of you do not like phonies? That's a better question. Raise your hand." And invariably, everyone raises a hand. So then I look at them real seriously and say, "You just sealed up the possibility of your ever growing."

The fact is that when we start to change, even for the better, it's easy to feel like a hypocrite. Doing things differently will feel strange for about thirty days, until they become new habits. And that feeling can add to the discomfort of making changes; we might even think it's more godly not to act inconsistently with "what we are." *Should I be trying to talk myself into believing God loves me,* we might ask, *when I don't really feel He does?*

The best definition of *hypocrite* I've heard, the one that answers that question for me, comes from my friend Dr. Paul Faulkner. Hypocrisy, he said, is pretending to be something you never intend to become. Put the other way around, if we're sincerely trying to become something better—more Christlike—even though we're far from doing it perfectly, it's not being phony to make the effort.

Think of it like trying to learn to play the guitar or some other musical instrument. In the beginning you pluck the wrong strings, you don't make your chords right, and you create a lot of disharmony. Does that make you a phony as a guitar player? No, it means you're striving to get better, fully intending to become a competent guitarist, and there should be gradual progress that anyone can hear.

It's the same way with developing healthy self-esteem and a godly love for others. The self-talk and loving actions will seem strange and even phony for a while, but striving to become all you can be for and with God, enjoying His love and passing it on to others, is what life is all about.

We can choose to be like the young man who came to one of my seminars and said his father never hugged him or told him he loved him, but that he was going to go home and do those things himself. He later told me it took him two days to work up the courage to leave his comfort zone and make the change, but when he did, it gave their relationship new life. Another man who had never expressed love very well went to his mother-in-law and told her he was going to start hugging her whether she liked it or not. She loved it!

An elderly Chinese lady, when she first heard of the love and grace of God, how He sent His Son to be her Savior, said in response, "I knew there must be a God like that somewhere." In the next chapter, we'll look closely at just how great a love this God offers you and me.

REFLECTIONS

"So how do relationships change for the better? Very simple. They'll get better when you change for the better. Most of the time we sit around and wait for the other person to change. We say to ourselves, 'I'll change when I finally see that he's willing to change first.' And you know what's happening, don't you? He's sitting in his easy chair saying the same thing about you!"

Willard Tate

Read Philippians 2:3-11 and 1 Corinthians 13 carefully and discuss the following questions:

1. *In what way did Jesus place our interests above His own?*

_____

_____

2. *What is the attitude of Christ that Paul is talking about in Philippians 2:5? Why is it important for Christians to have this attitude?*

_____

_____

3. *Refer to 1 Corinthians 13. List the ways in which one who truly loves is not self-centered.*

_____

_____

4. *How would this attitude help a marriage? A friendship? A congregation?*

_____

_____

5. *How does a person develop such an attitude? Where does he or she begin?*

_____

_____

Chapter 3

Experiencing God's Love

Have you ever been really hungry? Maybe you had a busy day where you started out running late and missed breakfast, had to work through lunch, grabbed just a snack in the afternoon, had to work through your normal dinner hour, and then rushed off to a meeting that night. You were so busy during the day that you didn't have time to think about your empty stomach. But finally, on the way home as you were beginning to unwind, you realized you had eaten hardly anything all day. Then you couldn't think of anything else! As we sometimes say where I come from, you were hungry as a *big* dog.

Or perhaps you've been sick with the flu for a few days, during which time you just didn't have much appetite. Toward the end of the week, however, as you began to feel better, your appetite came roaring back with a vengeance, and it seemed you couldn't get enough to eat.

If you've ever experienced hunger like that, you have some idea of how powerful the need for food can be. We know, of course, that there are many people today who are hungrier than you and I have probably ever been, and the television pictures help us understand even better how desperately the human body needs an adequate daily diet.

But no matter how hungry you may have been at your hungriest, each of us has an even greater hunger, an even more desperate need, and that's to be loved. Our need for love is a craving so strong that people will do anything to get it, and those who feel as though no one in the universe loves them are certainly the most miserable people alive, bar none. As a wise man once said, "The need to love and be loved is the simplest of all human wants. Man needs love like he needs the sun and the rain. He perishes without it. His basic longing is to be the object of love and to be able to give love. No other need is quite so significant to his nature."

"The need to love and be loved is the simplest of all human wants."

Now, God made us with that need for love, and what we really need is to be loved *unconditionally*. That is, we need for there to be at least one person in this world who knows us—with all our weaknesses, short-comings, and faults—and still loves us, someone who will go on loving us no matter what we say or do. That's the kind of love we all want, and we're never really at peace until and unless we have it.

Children of all ages want such love first of all from their parents. As another wise man observed, "A baby is born with a need to be loved—and never outgrows it." Unfortunately, the love we parents give our children is often entirely conditional; we love them when they're doing what we want them to do, but when they misbehave or do poorly in school, we run them down and make them feel they're not worthy of our love. I know because for years I was one of the worst at parenting that way. Of course, we parents don't usually intend to make our kids feel insecure or as though Mom and Dad stop loving them when they displease us, but often that's exactly the message we get across anyway. I'll have a lot more to say about this later.

Authors Gary Smalley and John Trent, in their book *The Blessing*, tell a story that shows clearly this need for parental love. They were counseling a young man whose father had served in the Marines and who very much wanted his son to follow in his footsteps. Well, the son joined the Marines all right, but he didn't really want to be there. So he became a serious discipline case, and before too long he was dishonorably discharged.

As you might imagine, the father was disappointed and embarrassed, and he reacted by cutting off all contact with his son. The young man moved to another part of the country with the feeling that he had totally lost his father's love and respect. He went on to start a family and build a life for himself, but as the years went by he continued to hurt deeply inside because of the lack of his father's love and acceptance.

Then one day the young man heard his father was dying. The son rushed to his father's hospital bedside, hoping desperately to somehow be reconciled to his father and be assured of his father's love before he died. But he arrived too late. And as he saw the still form of his father, he broke into cries of uncontrollable anguish, knowing he would never hear words of accepting love from the man who meant the most to him in all the world.

Even more basic than the need for unconditional love from parents, a spouse, or friends, however, is the need for a loving relationship with God. If we're going to talk about abundant life, about long-lasting relationships that make life worthwhile, we have to talk about the source of life. That relationship with our Creator tells us who we are, where we came from, and where we're going. To paraphrase the song, that's what it's all about, Alfie.

You see, if we know God loves us unconditionally, there's great security in that love. It gives us a healthy sense of self-worth to know that the great God of the universe loves us and accepts us just as we are. And then, having our need for such love met, we're free to reach out to others and let God love them through us. That, in turn, helps us to feel better still about ourselves and makes the world a better place for everybody.

Why We Have Trouble Believing in God's Love

Anyone who ever went to Sunday school can probably still sing the first verse of "Jesus loves me, this I know, for the Bible tells me so. . . ." Most people probably can recite at least the first part of John 3:16, too, undoubtedly the most famous verse in the Bible: "For God so loved the world that He gave His only begotten Son. . . ." We've heard countless sermons about the love of God, especially around Easter and Christmas time. And because of our need for love, I'm convinced we desperately want to believe God loves us. Yet the fact remains that most people, including Christians, find it difficult if not downright impossible to really believe that God loves them just as they are. Why is that?

There are probably many answers to that question, but we can focus on several major ones to explain much of our disbelief. The first is the one I've mentioned already, that we're raised to think love is entirely conditional. When little Johnny uses his spoon instead of his fingers to eat his applesauce, or when he picks up the toys and dirty clothes in his room, Mommy says to him, "That's great, Johnny! What a good boy you are!"

When he pulls his little sister's hair or throws a temper tantrum, however, Mommy says, "Johnny, you stop that right now! Bad boy!" And on a day when it seems Johnny has been doing everything wrong to deliberately provoke his mom, she's likely to say something like this as bedtime approaches: "Johnny, you little brat, sometimes I wish you'd never been born!" As Johnny gets older and goes to school, should he bring home a report card that disappoints his parents, he may hear Mom or Dad say, "Johnny, what's going on here? Are you stupid or just lazy? I never got less than a B when I was in school!" But if his report card pleases his parents, he'll get something like this instead: "Johnny, that's great. You're a good, smart boy, and we're proud of you. You keep up the good work."

The lesson all us Johnnys learn from that typical parenting style is loud and clear: love is conditional. If your behavior pleases people, they'll love you. But if you displease them, their love will disappear in an instant. You're not loved for what you are but for what you do.

A second lesson we learn is that what you do is what you are. That is, in our minds, neither parents nor children make a clear distinction between behavior and person, and the two become as one in our practical understanding. So, for example, when little Johnny buttons his shirt by himself for the first time and Mom says "That's a good boy!" Johnny makes the connection in his mind. "When I *do* a *good* thing, *I am good.*" And on the other side of the coin, when Mom scolds him for using his fingers instead of a spoon, he makes the connection, "When *I do bad* things, *I'm* a *bad* person."

In just that way, low self-worth is born in each of us, because all parents raise their children this way to one extent or another.

The next step in this process is to think we're unworthy of love. We become convinced in the deep recesses of our hearts that we *are* bad, lazy, ugly, stupid, or whatever. And then we think, often at the subconscious level, *"If people really knew me, how bad I am, they would never love me—never could love me."* So we spend our lives trying to hide the "real me" from the rest of the world.

That brings us to how we think God feels about us. Basically, we're convinced He could never love us. First, that's because we view Him through the grid of our parents. Very early in life, our parents seem like gods to us, so we think God is like them, and that impression tends to stay with us all our lives. And as we've seen, parents are usually judgmental and conditional with their love. We conclude, then, that God also is judgmental and conditional with His love; it's the only model of love from an authority figure that we have.

Second, we're so convinced of our badness and unworthiness of love that we can't believe God could love us, either. After all, if people really knew us, we think, they wouldn't love us, and God knows us in every detail. So He couldn't possibly love us, let alone unconditionally.

Third, unfortunately, some people have had bad experiences with God's people, and that also makes it difficult to believe in God's unconditional love. They've gone into churches, where God's love is supposed to bind us together, and found judgment instead of acceptance. Some have been stabbed in the back, gossiped about, taken to the cleaners. Then they think, *"If these are the people who claim to know and love God, He can't be a very loving God."*

How God Wants to Relate to Us

Understanding all that, how *can* we relate to God? Even if we didn't have trouble believing in His love, He's a spirit, and our lives are limited by what our senses perceive. We can't see Him, we can't shake His hand, and we can't smell His aftershave, if I can say that in a reverent way. He doesn't call on the phone or fly in from heaven to spend a few days with us, either.

Since we can't perceive God with our senses, how do we relate to Him? Well, He's aware of the problem, of course, so He gave us some pictures in the Bible to help us understand what kind of relationship He wants to have with us. The first of these pictures is found throughout the Word, including places like Isaiah 54:5, where the prophet said to Israel, "For thy Maker is thine husband." Jeremiah wrote in chapter 3, verse 14 of his book, "Return, faithless people declares the Lord, for I am your husband."

The apostle Paul wrote in 2 Corinthians 11:2, "For I am jealous over you with godly jealousy: for I have espoused you to one husband, that I may present you as a chaste virgin to Christ." In Ephesians 5, Paul gives instructions to husbands and wives, and then he concludes in verse 32, "This is a great mystery: but I speak concerning Christ and the church."

So the first picture is that God wants a husband-wife relationship with us—a close, loving, trusting relationship. He doesn't want some distant relationship like a king to his subjects or a master to his slaves. Instead, He wants warm, personal, continual fellowship with us.

With that picture in mind, we can understand that

disobeying God is not just a personal defeat or the breaking of a law. It's like breaking the marriage vow. And all sin is a sin against love. That's how personal a relationship we're talking about.

The second picture God gives us is also one of warmth and closeness. He wants to be a father to us. In John 1:12 we read, "But as many as received him, to them gave he power to become the sons of God." And in Galatians 4 we read, "God sent forth his Son, . . . that we might receive the adoption of sons. And because ye are sons, God hath sent forth the Spirit of his Son into your hearts, crying, Abba, Father."

This picture is painted most clearly in Luke 15, where we have the story of the prodigal son. There we see mankind's rebellion and God's mercy and grace, and we see how God is always ready to restore that parent-child relationship when we stray.

But note that there was also a prodigal at home. The son who stayed home and did all the right, socially acceptable things didn't have a relationship with the father, either. The one who went off into the far country and sinned was actually better off, because he came to a point of recognizing his need. The one who stayed at home never did see his need for a relationship with his father.

You know, there are people in the church who are like that prodigal at home. They may be song leaders or Sunday school teachers, but they've never admitted their need of a personal relationship with the Father. Please don't make that mistake yourself. Going to church faithfully and being respected by all doesn't guarantee by any means that you have a close relationship with the Father such as He wants to have with you.

Knowing God Loves Us

I realize that in spite of everything I've said so far, if you've come to this point in your life unable to believe God loves you, your feelings aren't going to change overnight. You may also need more than the biblical pictures I've just described to convince you that God does indeed love you, especially if the picture of Him that your parents gave you was strongly negative and judgmental. So let me offer seven brief ideas that have helped me believe beyond any doubt that God loves *me* unconditionally, with the hope that they'll begin to develop the same conviction in you.

First, it's good to count our blessings regularly, to keep aware of all the positive things God brings into our lives. As we read in James 1:17, "Every good gift and every perfect gift is from above, and comes down from the Father of lights."

Our natural human tendency is to focus on the negative, those things in our lives we don't like. But there are so many blessings we receive every day for which we could be grateful if we only stopped to notice them—our food, clothing, health, and work; people who love us, however imperfectly; a car accident we narrowly avoided; God's loving hand in the beauty and order of nature (see Acts 14:17; Rom. 1:20); the list could go on and on. If we make a daily habit of counting our blessings, it becomes progressively easier to believe God loves us.

Second, I've found that one of the best ways to feel God's love is to give love to others. The more I share it, the more I feel it myself. I'll have a lot more to say about that in Part 2 of this book.

Third, knowing that others love us because of God's love in them is a great help in accepting His love. Even if that love isn't perfect and unconditional, and even if there's just one person whose love we feel—a parent, spouse, teacher, friend, minister, or someone else— knowing that we're the object of godly love makes a tremendous difference. Indeed, if there's not at least one person in this world whose godly love we feel, it will be difficult if not impossible to really believe God Himself loves us.

Fourth, we have the record of how God has loved, cared for, and protected His people in the past. We can talk to parents, grandparents, and others who will tes- tify of His loving faithfulness over the years of their lives. We can read church history and biographies of God's saints and see His love there. We can look at the story of Israel in the Old Testament and see how He has loved and disciplined them like a loving Father over centuries of time. Learning how God has loved His people helps us believe the assurances of His love for us as well.

Fifth, there could be no greater, more convincing demonstration of God's love than Jesus Christ hanging on the cross to pay the penalty for our sins. When we let our minds dwell on that scene and think about the love that sent Him there and kept Him there even though He could have called on legions of angels to set Him free, we come to a renewed appreciation for how much He loves us. One time a man was grieving over the death of his son, and his minister came to offer comfort. "Where was God when my son was dying?" the father cried out.

"There could be no greater demonstration of God's Love than Christ hanging on the Cross."

"Right where He was when His Son was dying on the cross," the preacher said.

Sixth, we simply have to *want* to believe that God loves us. It's a decision, a choice we make with our will to accept His word when He says in so many places that He loves us. It's the same kind of faith that leads us to accept His offer of salvation. We must reach a point where our desire for His love is stronger than our doubts, where we say, "Lord, You have said You love me, and I want to believe. Please help my weak faith to grow."

---

*"We must want to believe
that God loves us."*

Finally, I would say from my experience that it *is* a process of growth, and we need to be patient with ourselves. Although I'm sure of God's love, I can't point back to any one event when lights flashed and bells rang and I just knew beyond any doubt that God loves me unconditionally. Instead, it's a conviction that's blossomed over time as I've grown in grace and knowledge and experience with the Lord, seeing His faithfulness and goodness over and over.

Like you, I, too, need to count my blessings regularly. We all forget and slip into complacency, and we all need constant reminders of His love.

When once we gain and nurture that assurance of God's unconditional love, however, it will provide the foundation we need for all our other relationships in life. It's the key to a healthy sense of self-worth. After all, if God loves us unconditionally—regardless of what we do—we must be people of value. God wouldn't send Jesus to die for someone worthless. It's also the key to being able and willing to reach out to others in life-changing love.

But as much as God loves us and wants us to see ourselves as His valuable children, the system of this world is very different. It works constantly to tear down our sense of self-worth, as we'll see in the next chapter.

REFLECTIONS

"You cannot reach out and help another soul without stretching your own."

Willard Tate

Turn to 1 John chapters 3 and 4. Consider the following in light of building relationships with others.

1. *What sort of love does John want us to have when he teaches us to love our brother?*

_____

_____

2. *Is the following quote appropriate for a Christian? "I love my brother in Christ, but I don't like him." Why?*

_____

_____

3. *In your own opinion, how is love perfected in us when we love our brother in Christ?*

_____

_____

4. *Now, let's apply this concept to the twentieth century. How does loving your brother affect: (1) A church division, when Christians disagree? (2) A disagreement between two members? Can one member sue another member?*

_____

_____

Chapter 4

The World's Destructive System

When people go to church, their number one desire, whether they or anyone else realizes it, is for someone to tell them they're somebody—they're important; they have worth. Everyone who walks through church doors is hoping to hear that in one form or another, and if the church doesn't meet that need, the people will go through other doors looking for it. I wish that the truth of the gospel and a desire to worship God were enough to bring people to church, but don't fool yourself thinking that's the case.

People are looking for that message in church because the greatest need in every life is to feel good about yourself. But we have to be careful to like ourselves for the right reason—not because we can ever be good enough by ourselves, but because God loves us and attaches great worth to us.

"Our #1 hunger is to be somebody."

Unfortunately, people end up looking desperately in various places for a sense of self-worth, of being somebody, because the system of this world works to tear down that sense of personal value, not build it up. So at this point we need to become aware of how that system operates.

It's difficult to like yourself in a healthy way and feel a sense of worth because the system, our society, constantly gives you negative feedback along seven major lines. Let's look at those carefully.

Why We Get Negative Feedback

First, the simple fact is that not everyone you meet in life is going to like you. It's just a part of living. That means that from time to time—maybe all the time—you'll have to deal with one or more people who just don't like you, no matter what you might do to try to be friends. I know some folks, including ministers and college students, who haven't figured this out yet. They think everyone should and will like them. They tend to get frustrated when they run up against that brick wall called reality.

Not everyone liked Jesus, the only perfect person who ever lived. Not everyone likes me, I guarantee you. And not everyone will like you. So that's one source of negative feedback.

The second reason we get negative feedback is that sometimes people will use us as scapegoats when things don't go right for them. It's called being in the wrong place at the wrong time—when someone else is looking for a way to vent his anger and frustration.

To paraphrase a Zig Ziglar story from his book, *See You at the Top,* suppose that a company president is upset by the fact that many of his employees are reporting for work a little late almost every morning, taking longer breaks and lunch hours than they're supposed to, and so on. So he calls a meeting and yells at everybody. "I tell you we're going to punch in on time here!" he shouts. "We're going to shape up or ship out!"

That very day, that president has a lunch meeting on the other side of town. It runs a little long, and as he gets up to leave, he realizes *he's* going to be late. Now he's concerned about what kind of model he's going to be if he walks in late, so he starts speeding across town. And sure enough, a traffic cop sees him and pulls him over. Talk about mad! He's not only going to be late for sure, but now he's also got a ticket.

So what does he do when he gets back to the office? He calls his sales manager and shouts at him, "Did you get that XYZ account? You've been working on it for three months now!"

"No, Sir," the sales manager says.

"Well, if you can't get the job done, I'll find someone who can!" And then he slams down the phone.

Do you think the president was mad? Well, now the sales manager is steaming. "I do all the work around here," he says to himself. "Why, if it weren't for me, this place would fall apart!" So what does he do in this frame of mind? He calls in his secretary and says to her, "Did you get out those letters I gave you this morning?"

"Not yet," she answers. "You told me I could give this other job a higher priority."

"Look," he says, "I don't want any excuses. Just get the work done. If you can't handle it, I'll get someone else in here who can!"

Now we've got three mad people. So how does the secretary respond? She calls the switchboard operator and says, "Look, all you do is sit up there all day and polish your nails. Why don't you come back here and give me some help with my work?"

Now we're up to four hot people, but by this time the workday is over. So the switchboard operator goes home, where she sees her little boy sitting in front of the TV. "Haven't I told you not to just park yourself in front of that thing when you get home from school!" she yells at him. "Get upstairs and change your clothes!"

On his way to the stairs, this mad little boy sees the family cat. "You've probably been up to no good yourself," he says to her, and he gives her a quick kick out of the way.

Now, one moral of this story could be that everybody would have been a lot better off if the company president had just saved some time and hard feelings by going straight to the switchboad operator's house and kicking her cat. But the other moral is that sometimes, you're just going to be in the wrong place at the wrong time and end up as someone else's scapegoat.

"More people die of a broken heart than a swelled head."

The third reason for negative feedback is that people don't want us to get the big head, to feel proud. And society has taught us that people get the big head if they're given too much praise and encouragement. A manager may have an excellent employee, but the manager says to himself, "I'd better not tell him what good work he does, or he'd get big-headed. He'd probably ask for a raise, too." You can be sure, however, that he'll let that good employee know when he has any complaints with his work.

That's the way most people think. But it's my observation that far more people die of a broken heart than a swelled head.

Fourth, as I've already suggested, most people have low self-images. They don't like themselves. Therefore, given human nature, they're sure not going to help us feel good about *ourselves*. They are not going to compliment, and may even criticize. When you're hurting, you want to see other people hurt, too, whether you realize it or not. As the old saying goes, misery loves company. We might add that it hates joy on the part of others as well.

Think about it for a minute. When are you the toughest on your children? When are you the hardest on your mate? It's usually when you're not liking yourself. And the closer people are to you, the more you take out your dislike of yourself on them.

Fifth, there's an unwritten rule in our society that says you can't say positive things about yourself. That would be bragging. "So," the subconscious mind says, "I'm certainly not going to say anything good about another person."

You see, we think we're in competition with each other. We haven't learned that you help yourself when you love and encourage others. We're afraid they won't say good things about us in return. Thus, the subconscious mind figures that if you build up someone else but you can't say anything positive about yourself, that will put the other person one up on you, and heaven forbid that that should happen.

The sixth reason for negative feedback is old bad habits—your own and those of others. We all develop these habits as kids, perhaps as a way to deal with the cruelty that other kids dish out so well, and in some ways we never grow up. As just one example of this, I developed into quite a smart aleck early on in my life. And only in recent years have I begun to get this under control.

Let's suppose I go out jogging one morning. I'm

wearing my fancy running shorts and top, and my snazzy running sneakers. After covering five miles, I come back into the hotel where I'm giving a seminar, and I'm dripping sweat and my hair's hanging down. One of the seminar participants sees me and says, "Been jogging?"

My first reaction to that obviously ridiculous but very common question is likely to be something like, "No, I just dress this way every morning, get wet in the shower, and head for breakfast." Or I might say, "Does a cat have a tail? Is the pope Catholic?"

Or suppose my car quits as I'm driving along the highway one day. I pull over, get out, roll up my sleeves, raise the hood, and start digging around trying to figure out what's wrong. Now, if someone stops to help, what's the first question he's likely to ask? "Having car trouble?"

And this smart aleck is likely to answer, "No, I just get out here and lubricate my arms like this every morning."

You get the idea. My bad habit is being a smart aleck. You and everyone else have yours. And they're the source of a lot of negative feedback.

Seventh and finally, we need to understand that the mind records everything that happens to us. The brain is the world's greatest audio and video recording machine. Somehow, though, it records life's negative experiences at a much higher volume than it does the positive ones. So when the experiences are played back, the negative memories boom out like heavy metal music from six-foot-high speakers cranked up to maximum. The positive memories, on the other hand, come out like whispers.

Psychological researchers have determined that because of the way the mind and memory work, we need to hear eleven positive statements just to counter-

balance one negative statement. That means that if
you're getting a fifty-fifty mix, you're falling behind in
having your sense of self-worth built up. It means that
if I tell you ten positive things about yourself and only
one negative one, you'll remember the negative long
after you've forgotten all the positives. That's a scary
thought, but that's the way things work.

Doomed to Be Losers

We've looked now at seven reasons why we often
get negative feedback from this world's system. But if
you thought that was bad news, hang on to your hats,
because it gets worse. You see, the system uses three
major criteria for determining if you're a somebody,
and by those criteria *most of us are losers*. That's why we
need to know how the system operates so we can
counteract its negative effects on our lives.

Appearance. The system's first big measurement of
whether you're somebody is appearance. If you're one
of the beautiful people, you're a somebody. If you're
plain or, heaven forbid, ugly, you're not a somebody.
You're a loser.

The world gives us this message loud and clear. It
comes at us from television, the movies, magazines,
advertising, fashion, the cosmetics industry, and
health clubs, to name just a few of the more obvious
sources. And we've bought the idea hook, line, and
sinker. Our society is infatuated with being beautiful,
with holding on to the youthful look forever. We're
constantly dieting, working out, trying new cosmetics
and hair preparations, paying huge sums for cosmetic
surgery, and doing anything else we think might
work, from hair pieces to fish oil.

Children begin to learn about the importance the
world places on beauty at a very early age. Just look at

some of the most popular children's stories and the message they convey. Look, for example, at the story of Sleeping Beauty. What's the heart of that? The handsome prince rides by on his horse and says, "Whoa!" He looks down at Sleeping Beauty and says to himself, "Wow, get a load of this!" Then he jumps off his horse and kisses her, she wakes up and they fall instantly in love, and they jump back on his horse and ride off into the glorious sunset.

Now, how do you suppose the story would have read if she had been Sleeping Ugly? The handsome prince would have seen her and said to his horse, "Get up!" and then galloped away. You see, the whole point of the story was that she was beautiful. Otherwise, the prince would have let her sleep forever.

What about the story of Cinderella? Again, she was beautiful. And what about her evil stepsisters? They were *ugly*. In fact, as far as you can tell from the story, they were wicked *because* they were ugly. Little children (who are very sharp people in case you didn't know it!) pick up on that right away. And very quickly they begin to equate beauty with goodness and ugliness with wickedness.

Scientific studies have shown what those stories and everyday experience illustrate for us. Namely, children who are considered beautiful get a lot more attention, especially positive attention, from others. It starts with parents, many of whom may not even realize they give better treatment to their physically attractive children, and it gets repeated by everyone else with whom children come into contact.

This human tendency to favor the beautiful can be seen in the Bible as well. For example, when the prophet Samuel went to the house of Jesse to anoint a successor to Saul as king of Israel (a story we find in 1 Samuel 16). Samuel, like a normal person, expected

God's choice to be one of the tall, handsome, older sons of Jesse. As each one went by and God said "No, no, not yet, wait," Samuel started to get frustrated. Finally God had to say to him, "Samuel, you're looking at the wrong things. I don't look at people the way men do; I don't judge by outward appearance. I look at the heart."

That's the way God evaluates people, and the more we can do that, too—the more we can avoid seeing people as beautiful or ugly and instead think of them just as folks for whom Jesus died, folks who all have great worth as a result—the more Godlike we become. This method of evaluating will affect every relationship in a positive way.

That's the ideal toward which we should all work. But in the present world system, beauty *is* a big deal, a major measurement of personal worth. And as I said earlier, by this measurement most people are doomed to failure. When some high school students were surveyed, for example, *80 percent of them* said they don't like the way they look. Since they know well and good how much value is placed on appearance, you can understand why so many teens have such low self-esteem.

We're all—even the most attractive people—also doomed to ultimate failure in this area by the effects of time. No matter how hard a person works out, no matter how much moisturizer and beauty cream are used, the wrinkles will eventually appear, the hair will gray, and so on. As Dave Grant said in his book, *The Ultimate Power*, "If we build our lives on the platform of our looks, we will eventually discover the platform is really a scaffold, and time is the hangman."

Proverbs 31:30 tells us that charm is deceitful and beauty is vain and fleeting. But there's another kind of beauty, an inner glow that God renews day by day even though the outer body is perishing. The apostle Paul talks about it in II Corinthians 4:16. This is real beauty, a Christlikeness that radiates outward to everyone around and that can grow brighter, not dimmer, with the passage of time.

Intelligence. All right, the system first says we're somebody if we're beautiful. Second, it says we're somebody or not depending on how intelligent we are. And how much do we need to know? The answer, it seems, is just a little bit more.

How intelligent you consider yourself to be depends to some extent on whom you're with. Around certain people, I feel rather intelligent, but around others I feel downright dumb. Unfortunately, I've often seen in groups where there are people both with and without college degrees that the ones without diplomas typically feel inferior and intimidated. It shouldn't be that way—do you think God cares whether a person went to college?—but that's the way it is.

Formal education and the degrees it bestows are in fact the official means of measuring intelligence in our system. It's just assumed that the person with a college degree is smarter than the one with no more than a high school diploma. By the same token, the person with the masters degree is thought to have it over the one with the mere bachelors degree. And the apex of this system, of course, is the Ph.D. or its equivalent.

Will Rogers had a good perspective on this whole business. "Everybody's dumb," he said. "Just on different subjects." I have a friend with a Ph.D., for example, who knows so much about cars that he tried to put oil in his engine by pouring it down the dipstick tube! Is he smart? When it comes to cars, he's clearly not the expert. But don't match wits with him when it comes to Hebrew, Greek, or Latin. He's a true scholar.

Which is the more important kind of knowledge? I

don't think you can say. They're both important in
their place. I do know, however, that when your car
engine needs oil, it's mighty important to get it where
it belongs.

When worth is measured by intelligence as defined
by schoolwork, the system has again set up most people to fail. Only the small percentage at the top of each
class are going to feel much self-worth this way. On the
other hand, kids who don't measure up by this standard will be crushed.

James Dobson tells the story of a typical boy called
Ernie who wasn't too smart the way schools measure
intelligence. The teacher says on a typical school day,
"Let's have some fun today. Let's choose up sides for a
spelling bee." Or maybe it's a math quiz. Whatever the
subject, Ernie knows what's going to happen, and he
wishes with all his heart that they wouldn't play these
games.

Now, without exception, who does the choosing of
sides for these games? Why, beautiful Mary and super-
smart Johnny, of course. They start choosing, and the
pool of those not yet picked keeps shrinking, and Ernie
keeps hoping to heaven that he won't be chosen last
today the way he's always been before. The pool gets
smaller and smaller, however, and Ernie gets more and
more nervous, digging his feet down into the floor.

Finally he hears Mary say, "Well, you can have him,"
and he knows exactly whom she means. But Johnny
says, "No, you take him." And the teacher, so diplo-
matically, says, "Ernie, why don't you come over here
to this group and help them out?" When Ernie's turn
to answer a question comes, he gets it wrong, just the
way he knew he would, and his team loses. Then he
sits there with his head down, wishing that somehow
a crack would open up in the floor and swallow him
whole.

Do you know any Ernies? I'll bet you do. There are lots of them. You may even have been one yourself.

What happens to the many Ernies in our school systems who get the message loud and clear that they don't measure up in the intelligence department? An experiment that's been done a number of times with fish illustrates it very well, I think. In the film, *Grab Hold of Today* by Dr. Eden Pyle, a northern pike was put into a holding tank, and then some minnows were added. Now, a pike loves minnows the way you and I do chocolate ice cream, so when the pike saw them, he made a beeline for them and gobbled them down.

Once the pike got used to this environment, all the remaining minnows were removed until the pike had a chance to get hungry again. Then some minnows were put back in, only this time they were in a clear glass gallon jar. Because of the reflection of the water, however, the pike couldn't see the glass. You can bet he saw the minnows, though, and once again he made a beeline for them.

Just as the pike was about to gobble that first minnow, *boom*, he hit the glass. He was a little startled by that, as you can imagine, but he gave it all he had a second time—*boom*. Now, as the pike did battle with this barrier he couldn't see, three things started happening. First, he began to hit the glass with a little less intensity each time he tried for a minnow. By the tenth and eleventh tries, he wasn't hitting it too hard at all.

Second, he hit it with progressively less frequency. At first his attacks went boom, boom, boom, one right after the other. As time went on, though, he got down to just an occasional peck, as if he were just checking to make sure the invisible barrier was still there.

Third and finally, the pike got to the point where he no longer hit the glass at all. He just swam around and around it. He was convinced he would never be able to get through it, would never get to eat a minnow again.

At that point, the experimenter removed the glass jar, allowing the minnows to swim freely around the tank. A number of them swam right next to the pike, some so close that they actually rubbed his gills next to his lips. *And the pike didn't even try to eat a single one.* He'd been conditioned to think he couldn't get them, and no amount of objective evidence could convince him otherwise at that point. If the experimenter hadn't saved him, the pike would have starved to death right there in a tank full of minnows.

Now think of Ernie again. He takes home a paper covered with red check marks. Actually, he'd done a little better on this one—he got thirty math problems right compared to just twenty-five last time. But the teacher, bless his or her heart, has been trained to focus only on the seventy answers Ernie got wrong, so the paper is filled with those red marks and not a single encouraging word. Ernie has hit the glass around the intelligence test of self-worth.

Ernie's dad doesn't know anything about building self-esteem, either, so he looks at the paper and says to Ernie, "You gonna be dumb like your old man all your life?" And Ernie hits the glass again.

Then he works hard on his homework. He really gives it his best shot. But he still gets as many wrong as right, and the teacher says, "Ernie, you know, you're the slowest student in the class." Boom.

This process only has to happen a few times, and soon Ernie, like the pike, will just quit trying. He'll reach the conclusion that he can't win. He doesn't know what went wrong, and he knows others can get it, but not him. The bottom line is that many a child leaves our schools with nothing but bitter, shattered pieces of self-worth. School is a dangerous place for a child with a fragile ego. And such a child will struggle for a lifetime to feel even a bit of self-esteem.

---

*"School is a dangerous place
for a child with a fragile ego."*

How many kids are affected this way? Another survey of high school students asked what they had learned best in school, and *80 percent* answered "I learned I was dumb." Incredible! If you're a parent, I urge you to reassure your child constantly that your love is sure and doesn't depend on how he or she does in school. But my main point here is that our system doesn't allow many people to draw a sense of self-esteem from the intelligence criterion.

Achievement. Finally, the third test for determining whether you're a somebody in our system is the biggest of all—achievement. And achievement is measured by the kind of work you do, where you live, the kind of car you drive, and, most important of all, how much money you make.

The thing that frustrates people here is that if you're trying to get your self-esteem from how much you make, then no matter how much you *do* earn, it will never be enough to satisfy you or anybody else. I'm convinced that the reason many salesmen don't do more business than they do is that they know that the more they sell, the more they'll have to sell in the future. And in their subconscious minds, they've got to leave some room in their lives to breathe. They've got to avoid having to meet impossible expectations.

Retired people have a huge struggle here, because the system says you've got to be doing productive work and generating a large income to have worth. And all of a sudden, at retirement, the person goes from being a producer to being a taker, a drain on the system. It's no wonder so many retired folks die soon after they quit work.

There's a scene in Marjorie Rawlings' classic book *The Yearling* that speaks so clearly to what we've been considering in this chapter. The book is set in rural Florida, and at one point friends and family gather around the grave of a handicapped little boy named Fodder Wing. There was no minister to do a eulogy, so one of the men of the community offered a simple but moving prayer.

"Almighty God," he said, "it ain't right for us to say what is right, but if we had been makin' this little boy, we'd a never made him with his back bent or his legs crooked. We'd a made him straight and tall like his brothers. But somehow you made it up to him. You gave him a way with critters. It comforts us to know he's in a place were his being bent doesn't matter no more. We'd like to think that you've taken that bent back and those crooked legs and straightened them. And Almighty God, if it ain't askin' too much, we pray that you'd give him some critters to play with, maybe a few redbirds and a squirrel or two. Thy will be done. Amen."

I'm sure God isn't nearly as much interested in how we look, what we know, or how much we accomplish as we are. And somehow, whatever undesirable features we have, God can straighten them out and make them perfect when we get to heaven. To the world they make a great deal of difference, but not really. Not to God, and not to His people.

Fortunately for us, God has made it possible for us to have healthy self-esteem in spite of the world's system, and that's what we'll look at next.

REFLECTIONS

Willard Tate said there are three criteria the world uses to determine personal worth or value: appearance, intelligence, and achievement. With this in mind, respond to the following questions:

1. Describe incidents where these criteria were used in determining a person's value and where negative effects occurred.

---

2. Read the following verses carefully and briefly summarize how each describes how God looks at mankind and how Christians should determine personal worth or value: (1) 2 Corinthians 4:16; (2) 2 Corinthians 10:3-7, 18: (3) 1 Peter 3:1-4.

---

3. Summarize how God determines a person's value. What are His criteria?

---

4. Have you seen evidence that God's people fall into the trap of judging others by the world's standards? What is the effect when we do not use God's criteria?

Chapter 5

Feel Good about Yourself

One day my wife, Bobbie, and I had come in from work, and she wanted to watch a Spanish-language station on TV because she was trying to learn Spanish. We couldn't find the little remote control box for the TV, however, so we started looking all over the house for it. Now, we've got a little dog named K.C., which stands for Kitty Chaser. So far he's lived up to his name real well, and he's just a little bundle of energy and happiness.

But K.C. has been known to chew up a few things, so when we couldn't find that remote control box, I began to have some visions, and they weren't of sugar-plums! Instead, they were of that little box, which the manufacturer insists is worth $300, all chewed up and laying out in the backyard somewhere. So while Bobbie continued to look in the house, I went outside to look in the yard.

I didn't find it out there, but then I remembered I had taken the garbage out not long before that, and it's such a little box, and maybe it ended up in the garbage can by accident. So I took all the garbage out of the can and sifted through it and put it in another can, but it wasn't there, either.

By this time it was starting to turn dark outside, so I

said to Bobbie, "Let's look outside some more while it's still light out. We can look inside after it gets dark." I got out my flashlight and shined it around the yard, hoping to pick up a glint of reflection off the metal, but I still couldn't find it.

Next we looked all through the house again, under the couch, under the bed, in the closets—everywhere we could think of—and we still couldn't find it. I said to Bobbie at that point, "I don't know. Maybe I missed it when I went through that garbage can. Maybe I should go through that stuff again."

Finally a light went on in my head and I said, "Listen. Wait. You know this morning we jogged, and the Walkman we wear when we jog is about the same size as that remote control. Maybe when we put our running stuff up in the drawer we accidentally put the TV control in also!" Well, we went and looked in the drawer, and sure enough, there it was. We jumped up and down and hugged each other, we were so happy.

Then I said to Bobbie, "I've got something to tell you that's going to be so profound you're not gonna believe it. Do you know why I couldn't find that box in the backyard or the garbage can or under the bed? Because it wasn't *there*! That's why I couldn't find it. It wasn't that I was a bad looker or a bad hunter. I wasn't doing anything wrong. It just wasn't there to be found in the places where I was looking."

"You can't find something where it's not,
any more than you can come back
from somewhere you haven't been."

Now, I tell that story because the same simple principle applies to our search as people for a sense of worth, for that feeling that we are somebody. The world tells us that we should be looking for it by trying to be beautiful, by being more intelligent than others, or by making more money or having a more glamorous job than others. But as we've already discussed, the vast majority of us aren't ever going to measure up by those standards. For the average person—that is, for most of us—the sense of worth we need just isn't to be found in those areas.

That raises the question, then, Is there a way for the average person with bumps and freckles and warts and a little extra weight and no college degree and no big achievements and a skimpy bank balance to feel good about himself? Or is that the impossible dream? Well, the world would say there's no way for that person to win, to feel good about himself. But I'm here to tell you there *is* a way. Yes, there is a way if we can believe three things.

Our Worth Is a Gift

The first thing we need to believe if we're going to have a solid sense of self-worth is that our worth is a gift from God, who loves us. It's something He gives us because He cares so much for us and about us. We see it in Bible verses like Romans 5:8, where it says, "But God demonstrates His own love toward us, in that while we were still sinners, Christ died for us." While we were still rebelling against Him, He gave us Jesus to be our Savior.

"Your self-worth is a gift."

We see His love in the story of the prodigal son in Luke 15, where we learn that He is always standing

ready to welcome us back into His fellowship whenever we turn toward Him.

We see it in the book of First John, where we read,
"Behold what manner of love the Father has bestowed
on us, that we should be called children of God! . . .
By this we know love, because He laid down His life
for us. . . . In this the love of God was manifested toward us, that God has sent His only begotten Son into
the world, that we might live through Him. In this is
love, not that we loved God, but that He loved us and
sent His Son to be the propitiation for our sins. Be-
loved, if God so loved us, we also ought to love one
another. . . . We love Him because He first loved us."

In Galatians 4 we read, "But when the fullness of the
time had come, God sent forth His Son . . . to redeem
those who were under the law, that we might receive
the adoption as sons. And because you are sons, God
has sent forth the Spirit of His Son into your hearts,
crying out, 'Abba, Father!'"

God loves us so much that He not only provided a
way of salvation, but also adopted us as His children,
sons and daughters, joint heirs of the kingdom with
Jesus, as it says in Romans 8. Now, I ask you, would
God love us that way and make us His children if we
were worthless? Of course not! In His eyes we have
such great worth that sending Jesus to the cross was
not too high a price to pay to save us, and He knows us
better than anyone.

And since God has given us that worth as a gift, it
also means we don't have to earn worth. We cannot
determine our worth in any other way. Any other
method is not dependable. All the work and the worry
we put into trying to prove our worth isn't necessary
anymore if we'll just recognize what God has already
given us.

You know, everything we do in life, we do for one of
two reasons, and both of them are related to love and

that sense of self-worth we crave. We do things either
to try to *earn* a little more love and sense of worth, or
we do things because we know we're *already* loved and
have worth and we're responding to that love. There's
a big difference between those two motivations, a
world of difference. The difference is called joy.

---

*"We do things either to try to earn love
or we do things because we are loved."*

The same thing is true of salvation. See, God has
built into all of us a basic understanding of our sin-
fulness and His holiness, so people everywhere know
even before they hear the gospel that there's a holy
God and they've got to get on good terms with Him
somehow. So in everything people do, they're either
trying to earn God's favor, or else they're responding
to the wonderful knowledge that He's given it to them
as a gift bought by the blood of Jesus. We cannot *earn*
God's favor, or our salvation. Our salvation is a gift
earned by Jesus. We can only *respond* and accept His
favor by a submitted life according to His word. Repen-
tance and obedience are simply the response of a submitted life.

A word of caution is in order at this point. Let's not
confuse the healthy sense of self-worth given by God
with the attitude promoted by the big self-esteem
movement that's been so popular since the late 1960s.
As a result of the teaching of that movement, it's easy
for a person to conclude that if I can ever get to liking
myself and believing in myself, that's all I need to suc-
ceed in life. But the truth is that you can get to heaven
even if you don't like yourself, and on the other side of
the coin, liking yourself is certainly no guarantee that
you'll get to heaven.

Now, the really scary thing about the self-esteem movement is that if you get to liking yourself and the way you are along the lines it teaches, the logical progression of thought takes you to the point of believing you don't need a Savior. *I'm Okay, You're Okay* was the title of one hugely successful book. And if we're okay, why do we need Jesus? Well, the truth is that apart from Jesus, I'm *not* okay, and neither are you.

The appeal of the self-esteem teaching plays right into one of our greatest weaknesses as people. We hate to admit we're needy. We want to be independent and self-sufficient. We want to think we can make it on our own. In terms of relating to God, people ever since Cain, who offered an unacceptable sacrifice to the Lord, have wanted to think they could work hard enough or be good enough by themselves to earn God's favor. Oh, we want very badly to believe we're okay.

Such thinking, however, flies in the face of Christianity. The heart of the gospel is that we are desperately needy people. We have a fatal disease, and it's known as sin, not lack of self-esteem. And it's only when we admit our neediness, repent, and come to the Lord on His terms for His forgiveness that we have any hope. Only a Savior will solve our most desperate problem.

Think back again to Luke 15 and the prodigal son who went off to the far country to live in sin. What turned him around? What put him on the road back to a restored relationship with his father? He came to the end of his own resources, both personal and monetary, and he recognized and admitted his desperate need. At that point he changed his direction—he repented and he was ready to be saved. That's why Jesus said harlots and sinners would get into heaven before some of the self-righteous people to whom He was talking: flagrant sinners like prostitutes aren't so easily able to deceive themselves into thinking they're somehow okay enough to get to heaven without a Savior.

We need to understand that because we're imperfect people, we'll never have perfect self-esteem. We'll never like ourselves 100 percent all of the time. It's unrealistic to expect otherwise, and to think that way just sets us up for disappointment and more feelings of guilt. So the key, I think, is to say, "Let's just like ourselves." In other words, every morning you can say to yourself, "I feel better about me today because of my relationship with Jesus."

The first key, then, in having a healthy sense of self-worth is recognizing that we've *already been given great worth* as a gift of God.

Learn to Love Others

The second key is to learn to love others, to let God's love flow through us so that other people will be built up and also come to understand they're loved and have worth. In Part 2, I'm going to be developing this theme of learning to love others and helping them feel valuable. But we have to understand first that we need to feel good about ourselves if we're to help others feel valuable. We can't give what we don't have, you see. You can't quench someone else's thirst if your own well is dry. So in addition to just needing and wanting to feel good about ourselves, we also need that feeling if we're going to be of much help to others.

What we give to others we get back multiplied, so the best way to feel good about yourself is to help others feel good about *themselves*.

Stop Comparing

Finally, the third key to feeling good about ourselves is to stop comparing ourselves to others. We must quit comparing! Did you realize that all inferiority complexes are the result of comparing? Think about it. How can you feel bad about yourself unless you're comparing yourself to someone you think is better?

"All inferiority complexes
are the result of comparing."

You know, a lot of people today think that the need to stop comparing ourselves to others is a great psychological discovery of this generation. But tucked back in Galatians 6:4 all these years has been an admonition we should heed: "Each one should test his own actions. Then he can take pride in himself, without comparing himself to somebody else" (NIV). The apostle Paul gave similar good advice when he said in 2 Corinthians 10:12, "For we dare not class ourselves or compare ourselves with those who commend themselves."

When we make the mistake of comparing ourselves with others, we're always going to come up short because we tend to compare our worst with someone else's best. And when we do that, we're always going to feel inferior. Else we will feel superior and become self-righteous. Both are bad because both destroy relationships. We just can't win at that game. The only one we should compare ourselves to is Jesus Christ as we seek to become more like Him, to develop more of His qualities in response to His love.

A New Motivation

There you have in pretty brief form the three keys to feeling better about ourselves. Now, does all this mean that we shouldn't try to be our best, that we shouldn't try to look our best and work as hard as we can and become as well-educated as we can? No, of course not. It's important that we do *all* those things. But now our reason for doing them has changed. We've got a whole new base of operations, and that makes all the difference in the world. Now we do those things *not* to try to *be* somebody, but because we *are* somebody.

"Now we can do things
not to try to become somebody,
but because we are somebody."

Operating from this base, my attitude is that I want to be faithful to the gift of self-worth that God has given me. I may even do more and try to learn more and try to look better than I did before, but now I'm doing it joyfully as I respond to God's love instead of anxiously as I try to earn love and a sense of worth.

Let's apply this to a little child in school. What we want to do is get down on his eye level and say to him, "Look. If you make all F's, I'll love you. In fact, even if you fail every class, I'll still love you. I couldn't love you more if you make straight A's. I love you. That's settled, no matter how well or how poorly you do. But you'll like yourself better if you are faithful to your gift." Now, I know young kids aren't going to understand that very well, especially at first. We have a hard time understanding it as adults. But if we keep saying it long enough, sooner or later they'll begin to understand and believe it, and what a revolution it can bring to their lives!

Unfortunately and much to our harm, we in America have made little gods of those three poor sources of self-worth—appearance, education, and achievement. But they've got the dust of death all over them. They haven't served us very well because they can't. Most of us have lived long enough to know you can't get life out of death. Many of those who have had all three of the world's values tell the story of thinking they had it all but finding they really had *nothing* at all. King Solomon in the book of Ecclesiastes tells that story. In our own age, look at the life of Marilyn Monroe, who had adoring fans and lots of money but was miserably unhappy. Check out the story of Judy Garland.

Think of Freddie Prinz, the young comedian who was such a hit in the TV series "Chico and the Man." At the age of 21 he seemed to have it all—money, fame, people laughing at his jokes, fans in the millions. Wouldn't you like yourself and want to live forever if you had what he had? Yet even with all of that, he was so miserable that he took his own life.

In spite of those examples, the average business person in the world today is chasing those three little gods as hard as ever. He's got his arms around his business and his house and his cars and all his other possessions, and as he gets older he hangs on tighter and tighter till his fingernails start digging down into the chrome. I want to walk up to all those people and say to them, "Oh, fellow human being, don't you know you're going to have to leave it all behind some day? Why do you hang on so tightly?" If you haven't learned to love other people and to accept love from other people, you are not going to be happy in this life—regardless of how much you know, how good you look or how much you have done.

I coached college basketball for about 20 years, so of course I'm a big basketball fan. And one time I was watching a game on TV near the end of the season, and Al McGuire and Billy Packer were part of the broad-

casting team. As they came on the air, Billy turned to
Al and said, "Al, this is the end of the season. We've
come to the end of the season, and it's kind of sad."

Then Al looked at Billy and said, "Billy, at my age it's
sad to see anything end." Now, he said that kind of
jokingly, but to most of us there was an undertone of
seriousness to it. Could he really be saying, "I recognize that my life's slipping away. I don't have as much
time left as I once did." And he was saying without
saying the actual words, "More than anything else in
the world, I want to live. I want to live."

When I saw that, I wanted to go up to him and say,
"Al, I know a man who talks about living forever. You
want what everyone wants, and Christ offers it as a
gift."

Another time I was watching the TV show "20/20,"
and they were studying cruelty to animals. They had
shown how several different kinds of animals are
treated, and then they moved on to cover chickens and
show what happens when chicks are hatched. They
put them on a conveyor belt and move them past people who are waiting to put them in boxes according to
size and color. If any of the chicks didn't make the
grade and get picked off the belt, at the end of the belt
they were dumped into a crusher.

Now, as they were filming this conveyor belt, it just
so happened that there was one chick that kept moving
on down past one box after another. Because of size or
quality or color or whatever, none of the packers took
him off the belt. And then, as he got to the end and
was about to be dumped into the crusher, that little guy
turned around and started running back up the belt! I
couldn't believe it, but he was running faster than the
belt was going in the other direction, and he was looking at all those packers as if to say, "Won't somebody
take me? Will you take me? Will you?"

Eventually, of course, the chick tired and the conveyor belt carried him down into the crusher. And as I watched I said to myself, "That's life. That's about as close as you can get to what happens. We're all headed down the conveyor belt of life, moving toward destruction." But Jesus said, "I'll choose you. I'll put you in my box. I'll let you be one of mine regardless of color, size, or anything else." That's good news—great news, in fact. That's the gospel. Jesus says, "I love you. You're special. I want to choose you, and I'll let you be mine." He'll never reject you if *you* sincerely seek Him.

REFLECTIONS

"If you don't know how to give and receive love, you'll never be happy."

Willard Tate

1. *Can you complete this sentence? "I believe I am loved because. . . ."*

_____

_____

2. *Why do some people have a hard time completing the sentence in question one?*

_____

_____

3. *The author of Learning to Love used several Bible verses that showed us the high value God places on us. What is your favorite verse? Why?*

_____

_____

4. *In general, does your congregation promote a warm, positive image of God or a cold, negative image? Explain.*

_____

_____

5. *How does Christians feeling good about themselves relate to teaching others about Christ?*

_____

_____

Chapter 6

Talking Your Way into Feeling Loved

There's one exercise I have each of my college classes do that's guaranteed to get the students' attention, and I doubt they ever forget it, either. I give them imaginary paper cups, and since I'm originally from Alabama, naturally they're Dixie cups. I tell them I want them to take that little cup, and then for the next fifteen minutes, rather than swallowing, I want them to spit into it.

When the fifteen minutes are done, I ask them to please drink what's in their cups. Whereupon they start saying "Yuck" and getting funny looks on their faces. A few turn a little green around the gills. So I say, "I don't see what the big deal is. You're gonna be drinking the same stuff in the next fifteen minutes anyway."

"Yeah," they answer, "but you can't be serious."

And I say, "When you get it out where you can see it, it's a lot tougher to get it down, isn't it?"

The reason I have them go through that exercise is that it is parallel to the way most people think about themselves. If our thoughts—what I call self-talk—were brought out in the open and looked at clearly, most of us would be disgusted. That's because most of us are putting ourselves down in our self-talk most of the time. We don't like ourselves; we think we're un-worthy, as I've been saying. In fact, if I were to tell you to your face what you typically think about yourself, you'd hit me! You'd say, "How dare you talk to me like that! Who are you to say those things about me?"

"When you get your thoughts out where you can see them, it's a lot harder to get them back down."

The Importance of Self-Talk

The nature of our self-talk is vital to believing God loves us, believing we're people of worth, and being ready to reach out to others in love. Did you know we're talking to ourselves about 80 percent of our waking time? You're probably doing it even as you read this book. You're thinking, *I hope my son remembers to bring his homework home tonight* or *I wonder what game is on TV tomorrow?* And you see, I can tell you that I think you're wonderful and special and that I really love you. But unless you're telling yourself that what I say is true—that you really *are* wonderful and special and lovable—my words will have no effect.

It's what you tell yourself that counts.

Fifteen college professors were once asked to reduce all the books about motivating people to action down to one sentence. Those professors, representing 200 collective years of teaching experience, were so intrigued by the challenge that they spent all day and all night trying to come up with an answer. And the rather lengthy sentence they came up with went something like this: Whatever the mind attends to, it considers; whatever the mind does not attend to, it dismisses; whatever the mind attends to continually, believes; and whatever the mind believes, it eventually does.

The book of Proverbs put it even more succinctly: "For as he thinks in his heart, so is he" (23:7). Put still another way, what we think about determines what we do. Or looking at it from the opposite side of the equation, our behavior grows out of and is consistent with our thoughts.

"As I think I am."
"As I think I am."
"As I think I am."

That's why our self-talk is so important. The words and images that fill our minds govern our actions. Words are that powerful.

In our society, we've tended not to think words are very important. We take them lightly. But the Bible, especially in the book of James, shows just how powerful they are. James wrote in chapter 3 of his book that the tongue (words) is like the small rudder that turns a mighty ship. By itself it may be little, but its effects are great. James also compared the tongue to a bit in the mouth of a powerful horse. Again, the bit is a small thing, yet it commands great strength.

"Words are the most powerful drug used by mankind."
                                        —Rudyard Kipling

The bottom line, then, is that if we're going to feel good about ourselves and feel sure of God's love and acceptance, we've got to take control of what we say to ourselves about ourselves. For most of us, this means changing our self-talk for the better.

Improving Our Self-Talk

Most people, however, don't even think about what they're thinking about. They're not aware of their self-talk. So first we've got to become aware of what's running through our mind. We've got to put a watchman at the gate of our thoughts.

My suggestion, which is the same one I give my college students, is to start writing down your self-talk so you can analyze it. At various times during the day—perhaps at set times or perhaps as you find yourself in different situations (at home, on the job, in the car, in the store, etc.)—stop and take note of what you're saying to yourself about yourself. Write it down in a notebook. This exercise will probably convince you of the miserable state of your self-talk much more than my telling you about it ever will.

Once you have some idea of what your self-talk is like, it's time to begin changing it for the better. And it's actually rather easy to revolutionize your self-talk. Take a 3x5 index card or a similar size piece of paper—something you can easily carry around with you—and write on it in big, bold letters, "God loves me." Then on the other side write in the same size, "Child of the King."

Now take that card with you wherever you go, and read it over and over again, every chance you get. Read it a thousand times a day if you can. Let its messages soak down into your subconscious and not just stay up in your intellect. Say the words to yourself repeatedly: God loves me. God loves me. I want you to begin to believe it with every fiber of your being. I'm a child of the King, a child of the King.

What we're doing is breaking in on the cycle of thought feeding action and action feeding thought, of action that's consistent with self-talk and that in turn reinforces and more deeply ingrains the self-talk. We're steadily replacing the negative self-talk with positive ideas, knowing that when the thoughts change, the actions will follow. It's not an overnight phenomenon, but a gradual, powerful process, much like the way wind and water shape even the hardest rock.

"The mind must manage the mind."

In fact, if you dwell on "God loves me" and "Child of the King" and really start to believe them, breathing in those great but simple truths, you'll be amazed how they change your relationships. Now you'll feel more of the warmth of God's love. When someone is rude, instead of being hurt, you'll be dwelling on the marvelous fact that God loves you. You won't need to retaliate. You'll be breathing God's love back out onto others. You'll find yourself liking yourself better, all right, and you'll also begin to see an improvement in every other relationship.

And now, in Part 2, we're ready to look at how we become channels of that love to a desperately love-starved world.

REFLECTIONS

"If I were to tell you to your face what you typically
think about yourself, you'd hit me!"

Willard Tate

1. *Have you ever heard anyone say, "I'm never any good at
games," or "I'll never be able to get this through my skull," or "You
know me! I'm Mr. Clumsy." What do these statements tell you
about the person speaking? Explain.*

_____

_____

2. *Restate Proverbs 23:7 (KJV) in your own words.*

_____

_____

3. *A counselor once said that what he found frustrating about
counselling was the great amount of time it took to help a person
think differently toward himself. He said that unless the one being
counseled could learn to talk to himself or herself differently, improvement was unlikely. Do you agree with this observation? Explain.*

_____

_____

4. *It has been said that we are in a battle over who or what
dominates the mind. Read Philippians 4:4-9. Make a list of the
things Paul says we should focus our minds on. By each item give a
practical example of that particular item. How would this change us
if we practiced this verse faithfully?*

_____

_____

PART 2

Reaching Out
to Others in Love

Chapter 7

Give Total Acceptance

Would you like to begin to change the world right where you are, in your little corner? Would you like to make this earth a better place to live? And would you like to know how you can do great evangelistic work even if you can't say a word in public?

The way you can do all those things is to help other people feel they're somebody, they're valuable, they have worth that they don't need to beg, steal, or buy. If we can get people to understand and accept that, the way we're growing in our understanding and acceptance of our own worth, we can change the home, the church, the workplace, and other relationships of all kinds everywhere. In the second part of this book, I want to suggest four ways you can convey that sense of worth to others and begin to revolutionize the world for the better, for Christ.

In this chapter I want to focus on the first of these four ideas, which is to give people total, unconditional acceptance. That is, we want people to know with certainty that we accept them for who they are and just as they are. No matter what they do or don't do, we'll still accept them just the same.

Few people ever experience unconditional acceptance, as we've seen in earlier chapters. Most acceptance and expressions of "You're okay" are conditional. "I love you" usually means "I'll love you *if* you do something" or "I love you *because* you do something." Seldom if ever does anyone approach a person who's in the middle of messing up and say, "You know, I really love you."

Children learn very early on that love and acceptance are conditional, based on performance. "You went potty all by yourself! That's good!" Or "You ate all your carrots! What a big girl!" That's what they hear, and the message is clear.

Known for Our Love?

In John 13:34-35, Jesus said there was one way above all others that people should be able to recognize His disciples. "A new commandment I give to you," He said, "that you love one another, even as I have loved you—all men will know that you are my disciples if you love one another."

"People don't care how much you know until they know how much you care."

The outside world looking at church people and church activities couldn't care much less what we believe. People aren't very interested in what we teach or the purity of our doctrine. What they want to know is how much we care, how much we love. If we can ever love and accept them unconditionally and convince them we do, *then* they'll be interested in what we have to say. The cliche that's so true here is that people don't care how much you know until they know how much you care.

That's one reason why Jesus *commanded* us to love one another, I believe—He didn't merely suggest it. He knew that the quality of our love would do more to attract the world to the gospel than anything else we could say or do. And that's why if your life is characterized by Christian love and acceptance, you can have a powerful witness even if you're not good with words. That's also why the church as a whole should be known as a place of warm, unconditional acceptance.

I remember once driving into a small town north of Dallas to present a seminar at a church there, and I didn't know exactly where the church was located. So I stopped at a 7—11 store that, as it turned out, was within an easy stone's throw of the building. I went up to a guy pumping gas and asked if he knew where the church building was.

"No, I don't believe I do," he answered.

Then I went inside and talked to the proprietor. He didn't know about the church, either. We had to look it up in the phone book!

Now, these guys weren't hostile toward the church. They just didn't know it existed! Amazing! Terrible!

Unfortunately, I've had that kind of experience more than once. But you know what I wish I had heard? I wish those guys had said to me, "There's a group that meets right over the hill there. I don't know what they are or what they call themselves, but they're the lovin'est bunch of folks you ever saw in your life. They take care of each other, and they reach out to meet other needs, too. You might check them out and see who they are."

Mind you, I'm not saying that the name you put on the sign in the front lawn isn't important. I'm also not saying that what you teach isn't important. But the fact remains that you won't have a chance to teach people *anything* until they know you love and accept them.

Jesus said that the entire law of God can be summed up in two commands—love the Lord your God with all your being, and love your neighbor as yourself. How is it that love fulfills the entire law—that is, the Ten Commandments?

"Love fulfills the entire law."

Well, the first four commandments deal with the supremacy of God, with showing Him the proper reverence. And what Jesus was really saying was that if we reverence God the way we should, that will turn into loving Him, and love will motivate us to keep on honoring His name, respecting His day, and so on.

The last six commandments have to do with relations with other people, and the emphasis here is on respect for mankind—respect for life, for purity, for property, for truth. And once again, if you respect, that will turn into love, and if you love people you won't kill them or steal from them or take advantage of them sexually or lie about them. Thus, love fulfills all the law as wrapped up in the Ten Commandments.

Now, if a society ceases to reverence God, as ours is doing, it will also soon cease to love and respect individual people. After all, why should we respect others who, as we've seen, are basically nobodies according to the world's criteria? The reasons we respect others are that God loves them and gives them value, and that He made them all in His image. But if society no longer reverences God, it will no longer respect what He made and what He values, either. Thus, if it's in my selfish best interest to kill you, why shouldn't I?

Lack of gratitude and reverence for God is the initial step in depravity and destruction of relationships. This natural progression of sin is described in Romans 1:21f.

On the other hand, love is like a glue that binds together all the other virtues that make it possible for people to live together in peace and harmony. Unfortunately, the virtues it supports—the compassion, kindness, humility, gentleness, and patience spoken of in Colossians 3:12—are seen as weak or feminine in today's world, and that may be another reason people so seldom receive unconditional acceptance and love.

Giving Acceptance

How can we make this idea of offering people unconditional acceptance practical? What message exactly can we convey that will get through to them? The key thought I'd like you to remember here is that the strongest motivational force in the world is to have someone who believes in you. Now, it's great to have heros and role models to whom you can look up. It's great to have mentors. But ultimately, nothing will motivate you more than to know that one person in this world, no matter who, really believes in you and your potential.

"Your strongest motivation
is someone who believes in you."

Some years ago now, I was in Alabama, coaching basketball at a junior college, when Wally Bullington, a friend and the athletic director at Abilene Christian University in Texas, called and asked me to consider the position of head basketball coach there. That opportunity changed my life, because I know beyond any doubt that Wally believes in me.

In fact, I'm convinced that if Wally Bullington were

to become the athletic director at the University of
Texas tomorrow, he would ask me to be the basketball
coach. I don't want the job, but knowing Wally believes in me that way is a tremendous motivation every
time I think of him, which is often.

Can you think of a specific person right now who
knows you believe in him or her? I hope so. I hope at
the very least that the members of your family feel that
way, because the belief and acceptance I'm talking
about need to begin in the home.

I was doing a seminar in a church once, and the
preacher and his wife were telling me about their son
who had been a real prodigal. He had left home, left
the church, left the faith—left it all. But a week before I
got there, the son had returned, and what a glorious
homecoming there was! There was rejoicing in the
family and rejoicing in the whole church. And it was
the memory of a good home that won the son's heart
back to his parents.

Well, I was staying in the preacher's home that week,
and I was admiring their dog, a huge, beautiful animal.
As I talked with the family, however, I learned that the
man didn't really like dogs. "No," he said, "that's our
son's dog that we kept for him while he was away."

And then the son said to his mother, "You know,
when I came back I knew you still loved me and believed in me because I knew you don't like dogs, yet
you never got rid of mine." The son knew, you see,
that in keeping his dog, his parents had been keeping
a part of him because of their love. They had been saying symbolically that their home was still there for the
boy to come back to.

That kind of acceptance is very practical, isn't it? But
in order to offer it to others, we've got to do something
that's talked about a lot but very hard to accomplish.
We've got to learn to separate the sinner from his sin

and hate the one while always loving the other. I'm sure that this son was doing some things his parents could never approve, yet while they hated his actions, they never stopped loving him. And unless we can likewise separate people from the sinful, harmful things they inevitably do, we won't be able to offer them unconditional acceptance.

"To love the sinner and hate the sin, you must separate the person from his behavior."

Let me conclude with one more story which I heard on James Dobson's radio program, and then something for you to do to practice giving unconditional love and acceptance. There was a guy who moved into a new neighborhood without really checking the area first, and it turned out that he was right next door to a man named Norman. Norman was real weird-looking, and everyone was afraid of him, so no one had anything to do with him. It was even assumed that Norman couldn't talk, but that was because no one ever tried to talk to him.

This new guy in the neighborhood, however, began to reach out to Norman. He talked to him when he saw him in the yard. He invited him into his home. And Norman started to respond. Amazingly, when the man took his family on vacation to Nashville, Norman went with them.

Norman had been like a child all his life, so they took him to the Opryland amusement park and put him on the bumper cars. But Norman didn't know how to make the thing go, so everybody else made him, the sitting duck, their target. One after another, they took their turns slamming into Norman's car.

Later the man said, "When I saw that, it occurred to me that that was just about the way life had always been for Norman. People had just taken turns hitting him emotionally." This man, however, was different. He didn't hurt Norman but instead loved and accepted him when no one else would. And the rest of the story is that before Norman died, he accepted Christ as his Savior, all because one person believed in him and accepted him and pointed him to Jesus.

Now here's what I'd like you to do. I'll bet you know at least one Norman in your own life, someone who's been mostly rejected by others, who's had the bumper cars of life hit him a lot of licks. Can you think of such an individual? And can you take the time this next week to just reach out and begin to give him some total, unconditional acceptance?

I know it won't be easy, especially at first. You'll be afraid, and the person may not know how to respond, either. Besides that, your friends might not understand. But I promise that in the long run you'll be glad you did it, and I also know there's almost nothing else you can do that will have a greater impact on this world.

There's a scene in "Dr. Zhivago" that illustrates the loving acceptance God offers us and that we can pass on to others. It was toward the end of the movie, and Comrade General said to Tonya, "Tonya, how did you become lost?"

She answered, "I was just lost." She didn't *really* want to say, so she went on, "We were running through the city, and there was a fire and sirens, and I just got lost."

"No, Tonya," the general said. "*How* did you become lost?"

"We were running through the city, and there was

fire and bombs—and Father let go of my hand. That's how I became lost."

The general answered, "Tonya, that's what I've been trying to tell you. Komaravsky is not your real father. Dr. Zhivago is your father. And Tonya, if he had been there, he would have *never, never* let go of your hand."

Likewise, God will never let go of our hands. Weak, sinful, and frail as we are, He still loves us. It's only *we* who sometimes let go. Our goal today is to reach up and take God's hand, knowing He will never, never turn us loose, and then to reach out with our other hand to take the hand of someone else as we all march together, helping each other toward heaven.

REFLECTIONS

Mr. Tate will emphasize four ways we can convey a sense of worth to others in these final chapters. This is the hard part. This is where we begin to put good intentions into dynamic actions. Consider the following questions about unconditional acceptance.

1. List some of the things which make it difficult for us to accept other people. Can you tell about a personal experience where you were first reluctant to accept someone and later found you were mistaken?

_____

_____

2. Christ commanded Christians to love one another just as He loved us. (John 13:34, 35). He said for us to love "as I have loved you." What kind of love is that? Explain your answer.

_____

_____

3. *Romans 12:4, 5 explains that we are different, yet we are also members of one another. How can we promote more understanding and patience between Christians?*

_____

_____

4. *Do you agree or disagree with the following statement: "When Christians learn to unconditionally accept others we will see the church reach out like never before." Explain your answer.*

_____

_____

Chapter 8

Give Unconditional Forgiveness

Revenge! When you think someone has done you wrong, that's what you want to get, isn't it? But do you know how difficult it is to get even?

In the college class I teach, I try to get my students to do rational self-analysis, to write down their thoughts and analyze them. Well, one time a young woman was writing down her thoughts, and I said to her, "Okay, what happened in your situation?"

"My boyfriend did me wrong," she answered.

"All right," I responded, "what are you saying to yourself? What's your self-talk?"

She said, "Well, I'm saying things like I'd like to cut the tires on his sports car."

"People do the oddest things to get even."

"I see," I said, trying to hold back a smile. "And how many tires do you have to cut to get even? Four tires? How about three tires and a tube?"

She hadn't thought about that, but if she was going to get revenge that way, she'd have to make a decision, wouldn't she? And what if she ended up cutting one tire too many? Then she'd have to live with the guilt.

Do you see the problem you run into if you're trying to get even? You can never balance it out exactly. It's futile to try, a waste of time, effort, and emotion.

In the last chapter, we saw that one way to help people find a sense of self-worth is to give them total, unconditional acceptance. Now my second suggestion is to offer them forgiveness, to let them experience real forgiveness, perhaps for the first time in their lives.

As we've seen, people don't get much positive feedback in our society, and that's certainly true in the area of forgiveness as well. Ours is a very nonforgiving world. People don't forgive or forget others' sins. Instead, it's as though society were saying, "We've got all your mistakes here on our computer record, and we're not gonna forget or forgive. You've got to live with what you've done for the rest of your life."

Fortunately for all of us, that's not the way of our graceful God. In fact, if I were to try to describe God in human terms, I'd call Him *the God of another chance*. That's because *every time* we confess and repent of our sins, He offers us newness of life and the opportunity to start over with a clean slate. He *does* forgive *and* forget. He puts our sins away forever and declares us pure, which by His mercy and grace we are. "As far as the east is from the west," wrote David in Psalm 103, "so far has He removed our transgressions from us." Through the prophet Jeremiah God said, "For I will forgive their iniquity, and their sin I will remember no more."

---

*"Praise the God
of another chance."*

Forgiveness and Our Children

Other people are going to seek this forgiveness of God *after* they've first experienced it from us. And the logical place for us to begin is, again, in our own homes. When we've wronged our kids, we need to be able to say, "You know, I made a mistake. I blew it. I was wrong. Please forgive me." That's how they'll learn to forgive, and that's what will free them to offer the same quality of forgiveness to others.

We don't do a lot of confessing to our children, but the results would be fantastic if we could learn to do it more. Maybe we just don't think of it. Maybe we're afraid it would make us look weak to admit our mistakes. But, Mom or Dad, I assure you your kids are already well aware of your faults. You can only gain their respect, not lose it, by admitting when you've wronged them and asking for their forgiveness. And there are precious few things you can do for them to better prepare them for life.

In addition to asking our children to forgive us, we also need to forgive them. They need a lot of forgiveness, of course, so we'll get plenty of practice giving it to them! I think God has arranged family life so we'll get lots of opportunities to let them start all over, don't you?

Unfortunately, many parents are a lot like the referees I used to watch during my twenty years as a college basketball coach. Zebras, we called them, because of their striped shirts. Now, the referee's job is to go around the court and find players doing something wrong so he can blow his whistle and stop them. And a lot of parents are like officials with their kids. You might as well put the shirt on them and give them a whistle. They just go around and point out what their kids are doing wrong.

Another thing I noticed about officials is that they never give any compliments for good plays—probably because that's not their job. But it's kind of sad, actually. And when parents have that mentality, it's bad news. I also never saw an official admit a mistake, either. Now, I suppose that on a basketball court a referee has to maintain a certain image, but if you apply the same mentality in your home, you're going to have trouble. Are you playing referee with your kids?

There's a monologue I love that summarizes these things pretty well. It's called "Father Forgets," written by W. Livingston Larned, and it's spoken in the voice of a father who goes to his son's bedside after the boy has gone to sleep. The truths in it are the same if we're talking about a mother and her child. And the father is talking about the day he spent as a referee to his boy. This is what he says:

Listen, son: I am saying this as you lie asleep, one little paw crumpled under your cheek and the blond curls stickily wet on your damp forehead. I have stolen into your room alone. Just a few minutes ago, as I sat reading my paper in the library, a stifling wave of remorse swept over me. Guiltily I came to your bedside.

These are the things I was thinking, son: I had been cross to you. I scolded you as you were dressing for school because you gave your face merely a dab with a towel. I took you to task for not cleaning your shoes. I called out angrily when you threw some of your things on the floor.

At breakfast I found fault, too. You spilled things. You gulped down your food. You put your elbows on the table. You spread butter too thick on your bread. And as you started off to play and I made for my train, you turned and waved a hand and called, 'Good-by, Daddy!' and I frowned, and said in reply, 'Hold your shoulders back!'

Then it began all over again in the late afternoon. As I came up the road I spied you, down on your knees, playing marbles. There were holes in your stockings. I humiliated you before your boy friends by marching you ahead of me to the house. Stockings were expensive—and if you had to buy them you would be more careful! Imagine that, son, from a father!

Do you remember, later, when I was reading in the library, how you came in, timidly, with a sort of hurt look in your eyes? When I glanced up over my paper, impatient at the interruption, you hesitated at the door. "What is it you want?" I snapped.

You said nothing, but ran across in one tempestuous plunge, and threw your arms around my neck and kissed me, and your small arms tightened with an affection that God had set blooming in your heart and which even neglect could not wither. And then you were gone, pattering up the stairs.

Well, son, it was shortly afterwards that my paper slipped from my hands and a terrible sickening fear came over me. What has habit been doing to me? The habit of finding fault, of reprimanding—this was my reward to you for being a boy. It was not that I did not love you; it was that I expected too much of youth. It was measuring you by the yardstick of my own years.

And there was so much that was good and fine and true in your character. The little heart of you was as big as the dawn itself over the wide hills. This was shown by your spontaneous impulse to rush in and kiss me good-night. Nothing else matters tonight, son. I have come to your bedside in the darkness, and I have knelt there, ashamed!

It is a feeble atonement; I know you would not understand these things if I told them to you during your waking hours. But tomorrow I will be a real daddy! I will chum with you, and suffer when you suffer, and laugh when you laugh. I will bite my tongue when impatient words come. I will keep saying as if it were a ritual: "He is nothing but a boy—a little boy!"

I am afraid I have visualized you as a man. Yet as I see you now, son, crumpled and weary in your cot, I see that you are still a baby. Yesterday you were in your mother's arms, your head on her shoulder. I have asked too much, too much.

One of the best investments you can make as a parent is to avail yourself of every opportunity for growth and development, and to expose yourself to the good material that is available. In my opinion, Dr. James Dobson is one of the top authors on parenting, and his books can be found in almost any bookstore.

Forgiveness in Marriage

The same principle applies in the marriage relationship. There was a very popular book a few years back that was made into a big movie, and it was called *Love Story*. The favorite line that came out of that book was "Love means never having to say you're sorry." That has a nice, sentimental sound to it, doesn't it? But what a lie! Nothing could be further from the truth. The whole essence of marital love is saying "I'm sorry. Please forgive me. Let's start over."

I believe this so strongly that I'll go so far as to say that *any marital problem can be solved if the partners are willing to forgive each other.* Let me turn that statement around to make sure you understand and it sinks in: I'm saying that a lack of forgiveness is *the only thing* that will ultimately separate a husband and wife and destroy a marriage. If, on the other hand, the ones who feel wronged can find it in their hearts—or in the strength of the Lord, if the feelings aren't there—to forgive, any marriage can be saved and then made stronger than ever. I've known of any number of marriages, for example, where one spouse was unfaithful, and because the other spouse was willing to forgive, those marriages survived and grew even closer than before.

One time a young man came up to me during a seminar I was giving and said, "Boy, I'm really having trouble with this forgiveness you're talking about. You wouldn't believe some of the things my ex-wife has done to me."

"On life's road, you arrive at peace by the vehicle of forgiveness."

I said to him, "You know why I think it's difficult for you to forgive? You think that if you forgive her, it's going to make her right."

"That's right," he said.

So I answered, "Don't you understand that forgiveness has nothing to do with rightness and wrongness? If she hadn't done anything wrong, you wouldn't need to forgive her in the first place." We like to think that by refusing to forgive, we somehow make the other person pay, but it's we who pay when we refuse to forgive and allow the cancer of bitterness to grow instead.

Forgiving Our Parents

The next group of people we need to forgive is our parents. I know I may be hitting you right where you live when I say that. During a seminar on the family at a retreat in the mountains of Colorado, (it was one of those terrible trips, you know, but somebody had to do it!) a man who was quite upset came up to me and said, "I'm so critical of my little boy. I'm always on him. He just never pleases me, and I can really tell it's affecting him."

"Sure," I said. "It's affecting your wife, too, because you're probably critical of her."

He said, "Yeah, what can I do?"

"Well," I answered, "I think you start by forgiving your dad."

He looked at me as if I'd hit him in the head with a hammer, and his eyes kind of rolled around two or three times. Then he said, "You know, that's right. Dad was always so critical of me; I never could do anything to please him."

"Look," I said, "till you forgive your dad, you're never gonna have any forgiveness to pass on to your little boy. That's where it starts."

I'm convinced that this need to forgive parents is at the heart of many of our problems. When we have any kind of resentment or bitterness dammed up against our parents, love and forgiveness can't flow through us to anyone else.

There was another time when I did a singles' retreat, and I knew I needed to deal with forgiveness. I started out thinking, however, that I'd need to deal with forgiveness toward former spouses because of things that were said and done during separations and divorces. But one exercise we did showed me the need they had to forgive parents as well.

We got in a little circle, and I set an empty chair in the middle and asked the singles to close their eyes. I talked quietly to relax them, and then I said, "I'd like for you to picture your mother or your father in that empty chair. Pull up all their features, their hair, their dress, their face. And then I'd like for you to go over and give them a mental hug." Well, I wish you could have seen the anguish and the anxiety and the straining and the tears.

And when the exercise was over, I asked how they had dealt with it. Over and over they responded with things like, "We couldn't do it. We couldn't do it." It was downright painful for many of them.

Even when it's difficult, however, and even when reconciliation is impossible because of death or some other reason, you can sit down, relax with music or a tape specifically developed for that purpose, and send thoughts of love and forgiveness to a parent—or anyone else, for that matter. Acknowledge the hurt feelings. Write them down if that helps. Recognize how often you've hurt God and how often He's forgiven you. Then send thoughts of love and good wishes, along with a mental hug. You can let that old ball of resentment just kind of take wings and fly away.

There's a book out that I highly recommend that gives some excellent exercises for forgiving your mom and dad and making peace with them. It's called *Making Peace with Your Parents*, by Harold Bloomfield, and it could make a big difference in your life.

I'm also convinced that we can forgive because God tells us to do it, and He doesn't ask us to do anything we can't do. That's why, no matter what's happened to us, no matter how horrible it is, we *can* forgive if we want to forgive. God will show us how and give us the strength if that's really our desire. He's not interested in frustrating us by asking us to do the impossible.

There's a great story about the need to forgive a parent in the movie "On Golden Pond." The language in the film was terrible, but it taught some wonderful principles. You'll remember that Norman and Ethel had gone to Golden Pond to spend the summer at their cabin, and their daughter, Chelsea, was coming from California for a visit, and wanted to leave her friend's son, Billy, there while she and her boyfriend went on vacation to Europe.

After Chelsea got back from Europe, she and her mother were talking as they walked down to the pier one day. Norman and Billy were out in the boat fishing, and their voices were echoing across the lake as they laughed and talked. Chelsea heard them, and you could just see the envy welling up inside her. She started saying things like, "Well, I guess it's better if you're a boy, isn't it? Dad never played with me like that."

After Chelsea had gone on like that for a while, her mother reached up and slapped her and said, "Chelsea, everytime you come you start this! You've got a chip on your shoulder, and it's not very becoming of you. Life's getting on; why don't you get on with it? Chelsea, your father is nearly eighty years old. When are you going to establish a relationship with him?" All those years had gone by, and Chelsea had never forgiven her father, and it had made a bitter person out of her. Forgiveness—it's so necessary.

Some of us need to forgive God, too. Most folks look shocked when I say that, but deep down many of us blame Him for our lot in life. Why did He give me the parents He did? Why didn't He make me prettier or smarter? God isn't really at fault, of course, but because we tend to blame Him we also need to forgive Him if we're to experience peace of mind and heart. He'll understand; just go ahead and forgive Him if you've been holding something against Him.

Forgiveness Isn't Easy

Now, I don't mean to suggest that forgiveness is easy. It almost never is, and often it's painfully difficult. It may mean giving up a long-held grudge or swallowing a lot of pride. But as much as forgiveness might cost, refusing to forgive is far more costly. It costs us peace of mind and good, loving relationships, time and energy, and maybe even our health. We would also do well to remember the command of Jesus, who warned us, "If you forgive men for their transgressions, your heavenly Father will also forgive you. But if you do not forgive men, then your Father will not forgive your transgressions" (Matthew 6:14-15).

How can we tell if we've really forgiven people? I have a simple but effective test. If we can think about them and wish them well, hoping they prosper in body and soul and find happiness, we've forgiven. However, if we wish the people misery and hope they fail in everything they try, we haven't yet really forgiven, no matter what we try to tell ourselves to the contrary.

I saw a sign in a shopping center once advertising the name of a hot dog stand, and when I saw it I said to myself, "That's the name of my next seminar." It was called "Puttin' on the Dog." I told you earlier about my dog, K.C. Well, K.C. used to run with Bobbie and me when we'd go jogging, about three miles or whatever. I didn't want to carry him much farther than that.

There were days when K.C. couldn't come with us, so I'd say, "K.C., you can't go today. You have to stay here." Well, he'd look so sad and disappointed. He'd tuck his little tail between his legs and just look miserable.

So what happened when we got back? Was he over in a corner, sulking, snarling, and refusing to have anything to do with me for a few days? No, you know dogs aren't like that. As soon as I had the door open, he'd be right there licking my hand and telling me he forgave me and was just glad to have me back. The same thing would happen when we were away for a week or two and had a neighbor feed him. As soon as he saw us again, he'd wag his tail and smother us with love. When it comes to being offended, he has a very short memory.

One night Bobbie and I were sitting around watching TV, and she looked at me and said, "Willard, I think I'm going to let K.C. be my example of forgiveness." And I thought, *How fantastic! That's exactly the type of forgiveness we need to extend to those who offend us.* So—when our marriage goes to the dogs, we've got it made!

"When your marriage goes to the dogs, you've got it made."

In a fit of anger, a guy threw a heavy stone at his dog and broke the animal's leg. And dragging the leg, the dog whined his way to his master, fell at his feet, and licked the hand that had thrown the stone. Friends, that's forgiveness, and if we can make a practice of it, we'll revolutionize our little corner of the world, and maybe a whole lot more.

REFLECTIONS

Webster defines forgiveness as "to cease to feel resentment against an offender." All of us have been offended at one time or another. The ability to forgive the offender has made relationships and the inability to forgive has destroyed them.

1. *Are you carrying a grudge at this time?*

_____

_____

2. *What is involved in forgiveness? When do you feel forgiven? When should you forgive an offender?*

_____

_____

3. *Read 1 Timothy 1:12-17. What light does this passage shed on the reason Christians should be ready to forgive?*

_____

_____

4. *Summarize, in your own words, the teaching on forgiveness found in Matthew 18:21-35.*

_____

_____

5. *According to the author of* Learning to Love, *"lack of forgiveness is the only thing that will ultimately separate a husband and wife and destroy a marriage." Do you agree? Explain.*

_____

_____

6. *Why is it so hard to forgive others?*

_____

_____

Chapter 9

Become a People Builder

Tell me, have you ever had anyone come up to you and say, "I've got a problem, and I wonder if you could help me with it. I'm getting entirely too many compliments in my life, you know, and there's got to be an end to it. I mean, it's just ridiculous."

That's kind of a loaded question, because I think I know the answer already. I've never had it happen to me, and I doubt you've had it happen to you. However, I've had the opposite experience many times.

In any audience I've ever addressed, I could ask for a show of hands of those who would like to receive more compliments every day, and if people are being honest, I'd see a hand up from each and every person. I'd have people all over the place saying, "Man, where do I line up? Give me a double dose of that."

We all want and need much more positive input in our lives than we usually get, and it's so important in helping people gain a sense of worth and self-esteem. We've talked about giving people total, unconditional acceptance and about offering forgiveness, and now the attitude I'd like to try to instill is that we need to be people builders if we really want to turn this world around.

What do I mean when I say people builders? Well,

first of all it means that I see people as the important thing in life, as worth fighting for. Most of the things we work and fight for in life—possessions and prestige and all the rest—aren't really worth fighting for when you boil it down, but people are.

Every Contact Important

Second, and this is so important, it means that I'm always aware that *every* human contact—every time two people interact in even the most superficial way— makes an impression. And every impression is either positive or negative. It either builds people up or tears them down. If we keep that in mind, in our families and whenever we go out in public, then life becomes full of opportunities to build people up.

I've been working on keeping this perspective for some time, so I can tell you this is true from personal experience. For example, once I was just sitting in a hotel lobby waiting for someone, and a hotel employee was going around cleaning out the ashtrays. He wasn't just going through the motions the way most people would, though. I've never seen anyone clean ashtrays with so much enthusiasm. He had a certain bounce in his walk that showed he was excited about what he was doing.

Now, I'd guess that most people in my position who had even noticed the guy would have smiled, and maybe even nodded at the guy. But that would have been it. When he came by me, however, I stopped him and said, "Man, you're doin' some kinda job. I can't believe this."

He said, "Yeah, I love my job."

I answered, "Well, you're not gonna be doing that very long. You'll probably own this place someday!"

He looked at me and just beamed with pride. With a few simple words, I had made his day.

I don't tell that story to make myself look good. It was a little thing I did, and anybody could have done it. There were lots of people going through that lobby who had a chance to make him feel good, who could have been people builders, but they didn't do it.

Another time just recently, I had lunch in a fast-food restaurant, and when I went to pay my bill after getting my food I gave the checkout girl some bills and change so that I wouldn't get a lot of coins back. When she gave me my change, however, it included a handful of coins. "I didn't use the change you gave me, I did it differently," she said. "Here's the change from your bills plus your other change back."

"I didn't want that," I said. "I don't want a pocket full of change pulling me over sideways. That's why I paid you the way I did."

The manager saw this going on, so he came over and said, "Oh, that's no trouble. We can take care of that." And then he gave me my change the way I had wanted it.

Afterward, all the time I was eating, I kept thinking, *I believe that girl must be new on the job. I think she didn't have the confidence in herself to make change the way I had wanted. And without meaning to, I've probably hurt her confidence.* So when I finished, I walked by the counter again and caught her eye. "Listen," I said, "you're doing a really great job! You have a good day." And like the guy in the hotel lobby, she just beamed in appreciation.

Again, this was no big deal. It didn't cost me anything, and it didn't take any more than a few seconds of my time. But it did require that I was sensitive to how even the smallest interaction between two people can have a tremendous impact on their lives.

"Look for opportunities to praise."

On another occasion, Bobbie and I were flying together to New Mexico, and Bobbie's purse was stolen. The airline representative in Albuquerque went out of her way to help us and put our minds at ease. So when we got Bobbie's purse back and the incident was over, I wrote a letter of appreciation to the woman's *boss* in Dallas. And he, in turn, wrote her a letter congratulating her for giving such good service to a customer. Now, how do you suppose she felt getting that kind of letter from her boss? And how do you think I felt knowing I had made her day? I got a lot of pleasure for the twenty-two cents it cost to mail that letter.

If we keep our eyes open for opportunities like that, we'll find them everywhere.

Let me offer a few brief guidelines for giving compliments: (1) Compliment the person directly and not just to others. (2) Look him or her in the eye. (3) Compliment the person for something he or she did, not something for which he or she isn't responsible. (4) Make it specific. (5) Keep it brief. (6) Be sure it's honest.

I must put in a good word for smiles, too. It's amazing the power they have to make people feel good about you and themselves. As just one example, a psychologist once gave a test to different students of comparable intelligence. He gave the same exam with the exact same instructions to two students at a time. The only difference in his presentation of the instructions was that each time he smiled at the second student as he explained the test. And the second student always got a markedly better score. Amazing! So let's be generous in our distribution of smiles.

You Get What You Give

The third point follows right on the heels of that last one, and it has to do with what happens to *us* when we work at being people builders. How do you think *I* felt after my compliments had made the day for those two people I've told you about? I felt great! Making their day made mine, too.

The operative principle here is that we get back what we give out. Another way of saying that is that what we give to others, we ultimately give to ourselves. This may sound simple, but it's about as deep a truth as you're going to hear. It's so simple that we forget it very easily. If we're sending out criticism, griping, complaints, and general negativism, we're going to get back criticism, griping, complaints, and general negativism.

---

*"What you give to others,
you give to yourself."*

On the other hand, if we're sending out a lot of encouragement, love, acceptance, kindness, and peace, we're going to get back a lot of encouragement, love, acceptance, kindness, peace, and happiness. Life just works that way. We might call it one of the natural laws of God's universe.

However, there's one stipulation I have to add to that. We don't just get back what we give out—we get it back *multiplied*. We get back more of what we send out than we sent out in the first place, whether it's positive or negative. We don't just sow a bushel of corn to reap a bushel. We get back more than we sow.

For a long time I didn't understand it, but this is why

people who always seem to gripe and complain have more to gripe and complain about. They've received back what they sent out, multiplied. In the same way, the people who are always excited and happy and looking for good things to happen seem to have more to be happy and excited about. Whatever you give to others, you're ultimately giving to yourself.

"What you send out is what you get back."

Bucket Fillers and Bucket Spillers

People builders are what I call bucket fillers instead of bucket spillers. Unfortunately, there are more of the bucket spillers around. These are people who go around with the attitude, "Some person, or life in general, has spilled my bucket, so I'm gonna spill yours. I don't want yours to be full if mine's empty."

That's a common human reaction to life, isn't it? And as I said earlier, it's a big reason why people don't encourage or compliment others. But if we want to help others and reap the multiplied benefits ourselves, we need to resolve to work at being bucket fillers instead.

Another set of names for these two types of people is candle glowers—those are the people builders—and candle blowers. The candle glower goes around helping other people's candles to glow as brightly as possible. The candle blower, on the other hand, doesn't like to see other people's candles glowing at all, so he goes around blowing out as many as he can.

I read a very touching illustration of the principle that we're giving to ourselves what we give to others in a book called *Man's Search for Meaning*, by Viktor

Frankl. Frankl was imprisoned by the Nazis in Germany during World War II, and he was stripped of everything—his books, his watch and wedding ring, the manuscripts he had been working on, and—most of all—his family. He had nothing left to live for except just the stubborn will to live in spite of it all.

Many people in his situation, however, didn't even have that motivation, and Frankl says they just gave up on life and willingly chose to die.

Some of the other prisoners would come to him and ask if he'd make a speech to all of them just to encourage them to hang in there for one more day and not give up all hope. Well, he said the last thing he wanted to do was make a speech, but he'd do it anyway. He'd tell the men to just hang on, that maybe when they dipped into their thin soup tomorrow, if they dipped deep in the bowl, they'd find a pea. That was a mighty slim hope to offer, but it was all he could realistically give them.

Well, by now you can probably guess what happened. Who did Frankl find was most encouraged by his little speeches? Whose hope was built up the most? His own, of course. What we give to others we're ultimately giving to ourselves.

Here's another way to remember the two types of people we're talking about. There are balcony people—they reach over the edges and pull up, or encourage, everyone they meet—and there are basement people, who pull everyone they meet down to the pits where they are. I want to be a balcony person.

Those basement people remind me of what a fisherman said once. He said he could keep crabs in a basket and never lose a one, even though there was no lid on the basket. Why? Because every time a crab started to climb out, another crab would reach up and pull him back down. I've seen a lot of people like that. Haven't you? I guess that's why we call them crabby.

Now, I can't honestly tell you that if you start looking for opportunities to be a people builder and giving out compliments, you'll immediately, every time get a positive response. Remember, people aren't used to receiving or giving encouragement. In fact, they're so accustomed to having nobody make them feel good about themselves that you might shock some folks the first time around!

But hang in there. Somebody has to start giving out the compliments so we can all start getting them back. Somebody has to get the ball rolling. And that somebody is you and me. I don't know how long you'll have to hang in there, either, but you will reap what you sow. I get a lot of compliments today, but I sent out thousands and thousands before I started getting them back more than just once in a while. It's the sort of thing that may start slow, but it will build.

Be Prepared

Here's another principle for you. I've talked about how we need to look for opportunities to build people up, and along with that, we need to have our hearts filled with love *ahead of time* so we can be ready to respond when we do find an opportunity. We have to prepare our hearts before we go looking.

My dad was a beautiful illustration of always being ready to take advantage of an opportunity to help. I grew up out in the country in Alabama, and we had a car, which a lot of other folks around there didn't have. When it got dark it was suppertime, and then after supper, very often Dad would say, "Well, I believe I'll run down to Partridge Crossroads and fill up the car with gas. Somebody might need some help tonight."

In those days, you see, the gas stations didn't stay open until midnight, and Dad always wanted to have a full tank before they closed. And then I remember as a young boy hearing people rapping at the door at two or three in the morning. Some mother's boy had been hurt in a brawl and needed to get to a hospital. Or somebody hadn't come home, and could my dad bring his car and help them look?

And the amazing thing to me as I grew up was that not only was Dad always *willing* to go, but he was also always *ready* to go. He always had a full tank of gas.

"Fill your heart with love
so you have plenty to give."

In the very same way, we need to be not only willing, but also ready to take advantage of those opportunities to build people up that the good Lord is going to bring our way. We need to have our tanks filled with love so we're ready to go and ready to give.

I think I've figured out something, and it's that even though we set goals and work toward them, often the things that happen in our lives don't come about because of our plans. Rather they come in *response* to our opportunities and our reaction to the situations in which we find ourselves. There's so much that comes along that we can't predict or control. But what we *can* control is how we react, and that's where our Christianity really gets put to the test. And what I'm saying is that we determine beforehand how we'll react by filling our tanks with love.

Setting an Example

Let me say a word specifically to parents at this point. The best way for our kids to become people builders is for them to see it in us, for them to have our example to follow. This means first of all that we look for and take advantage of opportunities to build *them* up, to compliment and encourage them. And it also means they need to see us doing the kind of thing my dad did—putting people ahead of his own comfort and convenience and yes, even ahead of his pocket-book.

That's a real challenge to us, especially since it's harder today than ever to pass our values on to our kids. Television, public schools, peers, and our society as a whole have a tremendous impact on them and may be giving them a very different set of values. And if both Mom and Dad work, which is often the case, their influence on the kids is even less, because there's just no substitute for spending time together.

It used to be that Dad and Grandpa and the boys would work together in the fields all day long, while Mom and Grandma and the girls would work around the house. That was a great environment for talking and living an example, for passing on family values. But for the most part, those days are long gone.

I don't have any easy answers for this situation. All I can say is be aware of the need, be an example in how you live as well as in what you say, and make time to be with your kids. Take them with you when you go places, especially before they reach adolescence—when they still want to go out with Mom and Dad. Let them see you building up that clerk at the store, that guy at the gas station, that bank teller or waitress.

Looking for Opportunities

Finally, let me encourage us all one more time to be looking for opportunities to fill a bucket, to make a candle glow, to pull someone up onto the balcony. We won't have to look far. There are fifteen to twenty million alcoholics in this country, each of whom touches four other people's lives in a significant way. That's sixty to eighty million hurting people right there. There are six million compulsive gamblers, and each of them touches four other lives. Three million young people run away from home every year. There's a suicide every twenty minutes, and in that same time ten unsuccessful attempts. There are a million divorces every year. Each of these lives touches four more.

It all adds up to a world of hurting people, many of whom live most of their lives in pain. But just that little spark, that little boost of encouragement from a people builder, can make all the difference to them. You can provide that spark, and what you give to others is ultimately what you're giving to yourself.

What It's All About

I was going to a meeting with a group of college football coaches and Jerry Wilson, the defensive coordinator, got there a little early. We started talking and I said something about the session, and he responded, "Yeah, we're just so bushed." I looked in his eyes and could see the fatigue. I knew it was just a week before full-scale fall practice got underway.

"We have new lockers that were supposed to come in three months ago," he continued, "and night before last they came in at eleven o'clock. We were up until two or three in the morning putting them in. Last night I was here trying to get the playbook ready to pass out when the players report on Sunday. We were up 'til two or three again. And if everything goes smoothly and we're fortunate, we might get out by three tonight."

"Jerry, is it worth all that work and late nights?" I

asked. I noticed he had a championship ring on his finger, so I pointed to that and said, "Is that worth it?"

"No, man, that's not worth it."

"Then what's worth it?"

He pointed to a student who had come into the lockerroom, then to another. "That guy sitting right there," he said. "That guy over there. They're worth it."

Jerry knew the worth of people. He knew that they're worth our best efforts, and I hope the rest of us can learn the same truth. It's *people* God made in His image, *people* He loves, *people* for whom Jesus died. And as we build them up, we build ourselves as well, and bring a smile to our Father's face.

REFLECTIONS

In a world of people-users, people-builders are always welcome. We see situations today where things begin to be more important than people. Willard Tate makes a powerful case for people building. Consider the questions:

1. Think of a time when you were built up by someone. Describe the situation. How did you feel?

---

2. What did Willard Tate mean when he called some people "bucket fillers" and others "bucket spillers?" Is there or has there been one of these "fillers" or "spillers" in your life? Describe that person. What can you learn from that person?

---

3. *Read 1 Thessalonians 5:11. What does this little passage say about encouraging and building up other people?*

_____

_____

4. *Read Ephesians 4:29-32. List some practical ways we can build others up and also list the things that hinder encouraging others.*

_____

_____

5. *Do you agree with this statement? "What you give to others, you give to yourself."*

_____

_____

Chapter 10

Learn to Express Love

Back at the turn of the century, there was something going on in orphanages around the world that was deeply troubling to authorities. Babies were dying even though they were well fed, properly clothed, and had no known diseases. No one could figure out what was happening. In fact, they didn't even have a name for what was going on, so they finally ended up calling it marasmus disease, which meant the kids were just wasting away.

Then one day Dr. Fritz Talbot went to Dusseldorf, Germany, where he visited a children's clinic. As he was walking down the hall, he saw a rather large woman carrying a baby. "Who's that?" he asked one of the nurses.

"Oh, that's old Anna," the nurse said. "When we've done everything we can medically for a baby, and it still is not doing well, we turn it over to old Anna. She's always successful."

That experience gave Dr. Talbot and other authorities the first insight into a key truth about human life, and it's that truth I want us to focus on in this chapter. Human beings desperately need loving physical contact. In fact, we can't live without it. We now know that an infant won't survive its first year of life unless it's touched physically and lovingly on a regular basis.

Thus, to cap off the giving of total and unconditional acceptance, the offering of forgiveness, and becoming people builders, we need to learn to express love in appropriate physical ways. We need to learn to hug, to shake hands warmly, to put an arm around a shoulder.

"You can't live without physical touch and you never outgrow that hunger."

The Value of Touch

Words of love and encouragement are important, but people need the physical contact, too. A lot of times a good hug will do more to lift a person's spirits than all the words you could say in a day. A wise woman named Kathy Tobin wrote, "Hugs are not only nice; they're needed. Hugs can relieve pain and depression, make the healthy healthier, the happy happier and the most secure among us even more so.

"Hugging feels good, overcomes fear, eases tension, provides stretching exercise if you're short and stooping exercise if you're tall. Hugging does not upset the environment, saves heat and requires no special equipment. It makes happy days happier and impossible days possible."

I've had a lot of people tell me they just aren't comfortable showing affection, but that it doesn't bother their mates. However, when you talk to their spouses and get down to the bottom line, it's always a different story. Sure, I know it's easier to hug someone in your family or someone who's been a family friend for years, but you can learn to hug others, and you can do it in a way that's appropriate and will meet needs as nothing else will.

A writer by the name of Sidney Simon says there's a hunger in America today that's greater than all the stomach pains caused by lack of food. He calls it skin hunger—that great, great need to be touched in a loving way. It's a need we never outgrow.

I remember when I was taking a psychology class in college, and one day the professor walked in and said, "My son has a birthday today, and he's twelve years old. I went up to him this morning and said, "Son, you're twelve years old now, and that means you're a man. Men shake hands with each other; they don't hug."

Our son, Mark, was just a little fella at that time, and I thought to myself, "That's great. Isn't that something? I can't wait 'til Mark gets to be twelve and I can shake his hand and make him a man. That's exactly what I'm going to do."

You know it's funny, but we also had a daughter Elisabeth, who was younger, and somehow I knew I needed to keep hugging her. What was the difference in the two kids' skin, in the two kids' needs? None. None at all. And fortunately, with the patience of the Lord and a lot of help from a good wife, I saw the error of my way and changed my mind before it was too late.

Today, our son Mark is a dentist in Abilene, Texas, and he doesn't hesitate to hug his dad anytime. You may say, "Yeah? Well big deal." To which I would say, "Yes, it is a big deal." I can't tell you how good it makes me feel to be hugged by my children, and it makes me feel even better to know they're not afraid to do it in front of other people.

It's also a big deal because I can't remember my dad hugging me very much as I grew up. It's not that he didn't love me; I knew he did. He just wasn't brought up to think that men hug other men, or even boys. And since we parent the way we were parented, I didn't start fatherhood as much of a hugger either. Now, though, that cycle is broken. We can learn and grow, as I have at least a little. Mark and Elisabeth also hug their children, and it will continue for generations to come. And so will I for as long as the good Lord lets me hang around. And that's really great!

We truly never outgrow the need for loving physical contact. After my dad died, I knew my mother was hurting, but I didn't know how to help. But on the weekends when we would go home, we'd visit her. One day we were sitting around talking, and almost out of the clear blue, totally unrelated to what we had been talking about, Mom looked at me and said, "Willard, if I just had somebody to hug me!"

I had been so blind, so dumb to her needs. If you had asked me to name her greatest needs after Dad died, hugging would have been the last thing on my list, if it made the list at all. But she named it first. There wasn't anything she needed more.

There's just so much power in a loving touch, in a good, healthy hug. We don't know exactly how it works—we just know it does, because that's the way God made us.

Several years ago, a social scientist by the name of Virginia Satir said we all need four hugs a day to keep the blues away, eight hugs a day for maintenance, and twelve hugs a day to grow emotionally. When she said that, everybody kind of laughed, and yet today I don't know of any social scientist or other person familiar with what makes people tick who would disagree with her. So use those figures as a yardstick to see how you're doing in giving as well as receiving hugs. And remember, what you give to others you're ultimately giving to yourself.

When a brother or a sister or a friend is hurting and you don't know what to say, just give 'em a hug. When a child is crying, what can you do? Take him in your arms and love him. You may have thought that was something to do only when there was nothing else you *could* do, but there really isn't anything *better* you could do most of the time.

---

*"Everybody needs 4 hugs a day
to keep the blues away,
8 for maintenance and 12 to grow on."*

A little girl arrived home late one day and told her mother she was late because her friend had broken her doll. Her mother asked, "Did you help her fix it?"

"No," the little girl said, "I helped her cry." She knew instinctively the value of loving touch.

Ted Sitton was the football coach at the school where I was the basketball coach, and one year he had a poor season. First, one of his top players died tragically at the beginning of the season. Then the team went through a losing season. As a fellow coach, I know what that's like. Unless you've been a coach you don't realize that it's almost like life and death, what you go through with the team. Finally, on top of all that, he got a call one morning saying his own son, Chuck, had died in a fire in a home across town.

I remember going to see Ted after I heard about Chuck, and he saw me coming. I never said a word; our bodies just fell into an embrace. We hugged each other until our bodies seemed to melt together. There was a communication there that was deeper than any words possibly could have been.

We instinctively know that many times a hug says

things that are beyond the ability of words to convey. We've just got to be careful not to lose sight of the power of touch to express love in that special way.

Especially for Families

Like most things we need to do and lessons we need to teach others, hugging should begin in the family. Your spouse and kids should be the first to receive your loving touch, and your kids also need to learn to do it from your example.

The best kind of hugs to get and give in a family are sandwich hugs. You get a piece of meat in the middle and a piece of bread on each side—group hugging, we might call it. Real family togetherness. But however you do it, *you* be the one to make sure everyone in your family gets four hugs a day to keep the blues away and eight hugs for maintenance and twelve to grow on.

Once after a seminar a group of us went out for dinner, together. Afterward one of the guys said to me, "Willard, can I talk to you?" I said sure, so we got in his van and visited for a long time.

Finally, after about an hour, he said, "My daughter is twelve years old, and it seems like we're drifting apart and having trouble getting along, and I wondered if there was anything you could suggest that we might do that would help."

I said, "Oh, I don't know. I guess I would love her a lot. I'd tell her how special she is. I'd tell her how much I loved her. And maybe when she's tucked in bed you can go in and turn the light out and say something like, 'You know, when the light goes out in your room, it seems like it goes out in the whole world because you're so special.' I think maybe I'd have some special dates with her, too, just the two of you, maybe go out to dinner. Also, I'd hug her a lot."

He looked at me, and his chin was quivering and his eyes broke forth like the fountains of the deep. He said, "Willard, why is it so hard to tell her? I know I love her. Why is it so hard to tell her?"

I said, "Because your dad never told you."

"How did you know that?" he said.

"Because that's where we learn our pattern of parenting," I told him.

"I never remember Dad telling me he loved me," he continued. "I never remember him hugging me."

"If you wait for emergency
to cause you to recognize your blessing,
you will probably wait too late."

This is very serious business. This man recognized he was losing touch with his daughter, both figuratively and emotionally, and it was mostly because he just didn't know how to express love. But we can learn. We can change for the better. I know, because I did it.

I ask my students to do interviews so I also interview people. I interviewed Dr. Jody Crumbliss when he had four children, the oldest of whom was 5, and he had no TV. Now, I figured he probably had enough money to buy a TV, but if he didn't we'd take up a collection for him. Either way, I wanted to know why he didn't have one.

He told me, "Well, I just decided I wanted to get to know my children, and my wife, too. I also made a promise to rock and read to each child every night."

I want to tell you, if we could get every father hold

ing his kids and reading to them every night, giving them that physical, loving contact, we could throw away the keys to the jailhouse. There'd be enough love and security and warmth there to solve all the world's problems.

While we're talking about the family, I also need to say a few words about hugging in relation to the disciplining of children, especially spanking. When my kids were small, I spanked them occasionally. And after I spanked them, I deliberately wouldn't hug them or give them any other signs of acceptance. I'd kind of keep them at a distance for a while, because I figured that if I hugged them, they'd think I wasn't serious about the discipline.

What a shame! If only I'd known better! When you discipline, that child needs more than anything to know that even though you disapprove of the behavior, you still love him or her. A little boy or girl desperately needs that assurance. So please, when you have to discipline your kids, follow it up immediately with a hug that says "I still love you; I always will no matter what you do."

Saying "I Love You"

Even though we should all be striving to express our love clearly and directly, it's also true that many people who have trouble saying the words have other ways of expressing their love. For example, one time a young man drove up to Alaska and made a lot of money over the summer working in a fish cannery. At the end of the summer, when it was time to go back to school, he drove all the way back home to Alabama. And as he pulled up to the house and his parents came out to greet him, his father's first words were, "How's the car running?"

That might strike us as an odd greeting, but it was this father's way of saying "I love you."

I came across another example in the play *The Curious Savage*. In it these people are trying to get their mother committed to a mental institution so they can take her money. But she wasn't crazy, nor did they get her money. But she practiced total, unconditional love and acceptance on the other people who were in the institution. One day one of the girls comes to her and says, "Nobody said they loved me today."

"Yes they have," the mother answered.

"Oh no they haven't," the girl said. "I've been listening for it. I would have heard it."

"Well, Florence told you this morning at the breakfast table. She said, 'Don't eat your food too fast.'"

"Is that love?" the girl asked.

"Why sure. There's a lot of ways of saying it without saying it, like 'Be careful, or take your umbrella, it might rain.'" And then the mother said a classic line: "You'll have to listen very carefully, 'cause most people won't be able to say it."

One way or another, we've got to let people know we care. We've got to express our love. A poem titled "If You're Ever Going to Love Me" captures this well:

> If you're ever going to love me, love me now, while I can know,
>   All the sweet and tender feelings, which from real affection flow.
> Love me now, while I am living, don't wait till I'm gone,
>   And then chisel it in marble—warm love words on ice cold stone.
> If you have dear thoughts about me, why not whisper them to me?
>   Don't you know twould make me happy, and as glad as glad could be?

If you wait till I am sleeping, never to waken here
   again,
   There'll be walls of earth between us, and I
   couldn't hear you then.
If you knew someone was thirsting for a drop of
   water sweet,
   Would you be so slow to bring it, would you step
   with laggard feet?
There are tender hearts all around us who are thirsting for our love,
   Why withhold from them what nature makes
   them crave all else above?
I won't need your kind caresses when the grass
   grows over my face,
   I won't crave your love or kisses in my last low
   resting place.
So, then, if you love me any, if it's but a little bit,
   Let me know while I'm living, so I can own and
   treasure it.

                                        —Author Unknown

Catch Them in the Act

Finally, when it comes to helping people feel self-
esteem and worth through the four things we've
talked about, let me leave you with one last thought.
As you go looking for opportunities to be an accepting,
forgiving, and loving people builder, don't wait until
you see somebody doing something exactly right to say
a good word. Instead, be glad to find a person doing
something *nearly* right. Praise people when they're trying to go in the right direction and you'll encourage
them to make it. Wait till they've already arrived and
many of them will never get there. Think about that.

Along the same lines, think about this: if you're better at reprimanding than you are at praising, you're

asking for misbehavior from children. Did you get that? Children will repeat the behavior that gets them attention, whether it's good or bad behavior. I saw great human insight coming from Dennis the Menace in the cartoon strip one time. He was sitting in a corner of the kitchen, and he had a little tear coming out of his eye. "Mom," he said, "how come I don't have a special place to sit when I'm good?" That's an insightful question, isn't it?

Let me take you back again to the movie "On Golden Pond." You remember how critical and bitter old Norman was, the character played by Henry Fonda. He never seemed to enjoy life, and he didn't want the people around him to enjoy it very much, either. On the other hand, Ethel, his wife, played by Katherine Hepburn, was so beautiful. She loved life. She'd get excited about a strawberry, a little flower, a sunrise or sunset. But Norman didn't see anything exciting in all that mess. He couldn't even hear the loons calling from out on the pond.

Then one day he was trying to light the fireplace, but he had the match backward and he was scratching and fussing and carrying on. Finally when he got it lit, he lit the whole wood bin. So here came Ethel and Billy, the twelve-year-old, and they pour water on the fire, and the water with the soot and ashes went all over the place. Norman turned to Billy and shouted, "You just made a terrible mess here!"

So Billy ran out on the porch crying, and he said to Ethel, "I wish he wouldn't holler at me like that."

But Ethel, so wise and tender, pulled him up and said, "Billy, he's not hollering at you. You just think he is. He's hollering at life. He's like an old lion, and he's just seeing if he can roar again."

Then toward the end of the movie, Norman had an apparent heart attack of some kind while he was carrying Ethel's mother's dishes out to the car as they were getting ready to leave the cabin for the winter. He was lying out on the porch, and Ethel was holding him and she looked up to heaven and said, "God, you don't want him yet. He's just an old poop."

Well, that experience seemed to soften Norman some, and after they pulled down the curtains in the cabin and shut the doors for the last time, they started to walk hand in hand down to say good-bye to Golden Pond. And this time it was Norman who said, "Listen, listen. The loons have come to tell us good-bye."

But my point, you see, is that he waited too long. He could have been hearing the loons all summer, and every summer before that. Don't wait that long. Don't let the good things you already have in your life pass you by until some tragedy comes along to make you enjoy them. You'll probably end up waiting too long if you wait for that.

A traveling salesman called home one day. And just as he hung up the phone and walked away, it rang again. He assumed it was going to be the operator telling him to put more coins in, and sure enough it was the operator. But she said to him, "I thought you'd like to know that just as you hung up, your wife said she loved you."

Did he need to know that? It's life changing. Would you have been the kind of operator to take the time to call the guy back? It seems to me that somehow God is saying to me as I write this, "Willard, tell 'em one more time that I love 'em." I thought you needed to know that, and I love you, too.

REFLECTIONS

"You be the one to make sure everyone in your family gets four hugs a day to keep the blues away, eight hugs for maintenance and twelve to grow on."

Willard Tate

1. *Willard Tate refers to "skin hunger" in America today. What does that phrase mean to you? Do you agree? Describe someone you know who needs more "touch".*

———————————————————————————

———————————————————————————

2. *List some of the incidents in the New Testament you can recall where loving and physical contact played a role.*

———————————————————————————

———————————————————————————

3. *Do you agree or disagree with this statement? "People don't hug and touch each other enough; they seem reluctant." Explain.*

———————————————————————————

———————————————————————————

4. *Should a church be a place where hugging and touching play an important role? Should the church emphasize it? Explain.*

———————————————————————————

———————————————————————————

Chapter 11

Loving Our Children

A friend told me about how he cut the grass in his backyard. His sons wanted him to play ball, but he needed to cut the grass. He said he'd pitch the ball, and while the boys hit and fielded the ball, he would make one cut around the backyard. Then he'd pitch the ball again and make another cut. Soon the yard would be cut, and the boys had fun playing ball. He said, "The boys won't remember my cutting the grass, but they will remember my playing ball with them."

Harmon Killebrew is one of the all-time great home run hitters in the game of baseball, and a few years ago he was inducted into baseball's Hall of Fame. During his speech in the ceremony, he told about how his dad used to go out and play ball with him and the other boys all the time when he was growing up. And then he told how one day his mom hollered out the window to them, "You're killing the grass!"

His dad hollered back and said, "We ain't raisin' grass, we're raisin' boys!"

I love that story because it illustrates so well some of the key principles I want to convey about loving our children. I've discussed the family throughout this book, saying that all the good things we want to do for others should begin in our own homes. But now I want

*"We ain't raising grass;
we're raising boys."*

to add a few more brush strokes to the picture of Godly parenting I've been trying to paint.

The Power of Example

One principle we can see in Harmon Killebrew's story is the power of example. Isn't it interesting that Killebrew remembered that statement by his father? It says a lot about his dad's priorities, doesn't it, and about what kind of impact his father had. My guess would be that with a model like that, Harmon himself is a fine father.

There are three ways children learn. The first is by example. The second is by example. And the third—you guessed it—is by example. The power of parental example simply can't be overstated. Albert Schweitzer was once asked whether he thought example was the most powerful thing in motivating a person to change. He replied, "No, I don't think it's the most powerful thing. I think it's the *only* thing."

A while back I bought a videocassette camera to record some of those magic moments with our grandchildren. But one day my son and I went out and used it to film ourselves playing golf. When I got back to the house and started looking at the tape, I said, "Hey, my problem is obvious. That's an old man playing golf there!" In a more serious vein I also said, "It's my backswing. Can you see the loop in there?"

How did I recognize the problem? I had been watching a professional closely for a number of years, and I had the picture of his perfect swing ingrained in my mind's eye. It was my model, and I could immediately recognize the difference between it and my own loopy swing. The power of example.

We need to realize that we're models to our children whether we like it or not. Our example will be positive or negative or, most likely, a mixture of the two, but there's no avoiding being an example. Children learn how to be fathers, mothers, workers, friends, and Christians primarily by watching their parents. Our only choice is what kind of example we'll be, and that's a fact we need to bear in mind constantly. It means that the way we parent is the most important factor in determining whether our children will grow up knowing they're loved by God and knowing they can have healthy self-esteem because God gives them great worth.

"Jesus is our perfect model."

Feeling Loved

That leads to a second principle we can see illustrated in Killebrew's story, which is that it's vital for children to *feel* loved. From the description of his father's words and actions, it's obvious Killebrew knew he was loved. He felt that love from an early age. Unfortunately, not all kids have that assurance. In fact, it's my conviction that most children do *not* feel loved by Mom and Dad—especially Dad. Why do so many children run away from home? Most of them feel home is a place where they're not wanted or loved.

At the same time, I'm sure that most parents *do* love their children very much, including those whose children run away. Ironic, isn't it? How can it be that parents love their kids but the kids don't feel loved?

Simply said, being loved and feeling loved aren't necessarily the same thing. There's a big difference between the two. And it really doesn't matter, in one sense, how much we love our children if they don't feel it. It's sort of like having a million dollars in the bank and yet living like a pauper; the money does no good if you don't know it's there for you to use.

---

*"There is a big difference
between being loved and feeling loved."*

This brings us back to the subject of the last chapter, the need to express our love. So many parents, especially fathers, struggle with that because their own parents weren't good at demonstrating their love in obvious ways. The father who talked with me in his van and said he was afraid he was losing his daughter because he just couldn't tell her he loved her is a perfect example. My own father wasn't very demonstrative, either, and I'm sure that's part of why it took me as long as it did to learn to express love to my own family.

Understanding the difference between being loved and feeling loved also brings us back to the importance of separating our children from their behavior. Discipline is certainly necessary, especially in the early years, and we can hold our children to high standards. But always our focus needs to be on the unacceptable *behavior or attitude*, followed by an affirmation of our love for them personally.

This is what Paul was talking about in Ephesians 6:4 when he said, "You, fathers, do not provoke your children to wrath, but bring them up in the nurture and admonition of the Lord." Discipline that comes across as a personal attack makes children mad and resentful and leads to the low sense of self-worth we've been talking about. But discipline that includes loving nurture of the child leads to the child's feeling that Mom and Dad—and the Lord Himself—loves him.

I must confess that I was one of the worst offenders as a father. So many times my discipline of my children consisted of attacks on them personally. I vividly remember one time when my daughter Elisabeth was a teenager and I came home from work and found her room in a mess. Seeing that, I chose to be angry, and when she arrived home a little later, I met her in the front yard and came down hard on her. I attacked her as a person, and not the behavior of leaving a messy room.

My son Mark got his share of it, too. Being a college basketball coach, I had high expectations of my son in sports. I was tough on him, not knowing enough to separate his person and his behavior when he didn't do as well as I'd hoped.

Another mistake I made was that as a young father, I wouldn't talk about my frustrations and irritations while they were still small. Instead I'd let them build up, then explode out of proportion over some incident or other. When that happens, you're bound to act too harshly and to come down on a person rather than keeping the focus on behavior, where it ought to be.

One night not long ago I was playing and having a great time with my granddaughter Amber, Mark's little girl, and Mark watched us for a while. Then he said, "Amber, this man playing with you is not the same man who was my daddy." To which I can only say that I hope he was right. I hope I've grown a great deal since the days when I didn't know how to discipline him.

Many people in my seminars, after I say some of these things, come up to me afterward and say they wish they'd heard these concepts twenty or thirty years ago. I tell them I wish I had, too. I'd have given anything to have known these principles when my kids were little—and they'd have given more. But we've all got to start where we are right now and do what we can. And by God's grace we can grow and our relationships can be made into what we want them to be as we begin to do things right.

Things Change When We Change

Doing things right—that brings us back to the truth that things change as we change. Our relationships get better as we become better people. Our children respond better as we become better parents.

A woman in Houston who heard me speak along these lines told me her little daughter had been a very offensive, strong-willed child. No one liked her. Not even she, the mother, liked her. "I didn't want to touch her or hug her. It was terrible," she said.

But then one day it dawned on this mother that her daughter wasn't going to volunteer to change, that she was the only one who could make any positive change in this relationship. So she made a conscious, painful decision to make herself love her child, to reach out to her and hug her and surround her with love regardless of what she did or how she felt.

At this point in our conversation the daughter came over to where we were talking, so the mother wisely stopped talking about her. But I was able to observe them for a few minutes, and I was struck by what a warm, loving relationship they had. Later the woman and I spoke briefly again, and she said to me, "You can see how much different our relationship is now." She had instinctively (or was it God's grace?) understood and applied a number of the concepts in this book, hadn't she?

Yes, relationships change when we take the initiative to change. The change isn't always easy and doesn't usually happen overnight, and I can't even guarantee that the change will always be positive. But I can guarantee that until we're willing to change for the better, our relationships will remain the same or get worse.

Parental Goals

Let me summarize at this point what some of our goals as parents are to be as I understand them. First, we want to instill in our children the truth that God loves them unconditionally. This has a direct application to what we teach through words, of course, but again, our example is far more important in conveying this.

Second, we want to teach them that God is for them. He wants only what's best for them. He's not looking to catch them doing something wrong but a loving Father who wants to bless them and see them lead fulfilled, joyful lives. Once again, our example is the principal teacher.

Third, God forgives. He's the God of another chance. And how will our children learn that? You know the answer.

Fourth, we want our children to gain self-esteem by the way we discipline, about which I've said much. We want to them to feel, "I'm loved. I have worth because I'm made in God's image. I'm too valuable a person to choose to mess up."

Fifth, we want through our discipline for our kids to become *self*-disciplined. The more they like themselves, the more they like to behave properly and the more they'll grow into disciplined adults who do what they need to do when they need to do it without being told and without being watched every minute.

If we discipline our children for any reason other than to develop their self-esteem and to help them become self-disciplined, it's for the wrong reason. Satisfying our own ego or meeting our own needs or winning a battle isn't good enough. Again, I confess that I'm urging the opposite of the way I raised my kids for many years, but I learned and grew, and so can you.

The One-Minute Parent

There's a book I have to recommend called *The One-Minute Parent*, by Spencer Johnson. The book is so good that I'd even buy it before I bought bread for my family; it can be that beneficial to your family. In it he suggests that a lot of good parenting can happen in little one-minute segments. For example, his name for the kind of discipline I've been talking about is "the one-minute reprimand." You reprimand the kid's unacceptable behavior, and then you give him a hug and an "I love you." Nothing fancy or long and drawn out, but terribly effective.

However, the best thing to do, the most powerful way to develop self-discipline, is to watch for a child doing something right—or nearly right—and give him a one-minute praising *before* he gets into objectionable behavior. If we'll look for good intentions and attempts to do things right, even if the results don't quite work out, we can catch a kid doing something nearly right almost all the time. Then you take him by the shoulders, look him in the eye, tell him specifically what he did that you appreciate, tell him how you feel about it, take a big breath so the praise can sink in a little, and then give him a big hug.

A one-minute praising might go something like this: "Mark, come here a minute." You squat down so you're at his level and looking him straight in the eye. "Son, I saw you try to tie your sister's shoe for her. That was a very nice thing to do, and it made me very proud of you for being so helpful. (Pause) Let me give you a big hug!" Believe me, you'll both love it.

The reason that approach is so powerful is that children have to have attention, as we all do. And they'll get it any way they can. If they don't get it for doing something positive, they'll do something negative for it. That means it's a good idea for us to evaluate ourselves to see if we're better at reprimanding or praising. If we're better at reprimanding, we're asking for misbehavior, because our kids will quickly learn that that's the best way to get attention. Our tendency is to ignore our kids when they're not messing up, but that's just when we should be looking for opportunities for one-minute praisings.

Finally, as one-minute parents, we want to help our children set simple, brief personal goals for their behavior. This can begin when they're very young. "I'll pick up my toys. I'll put my dirty clothes in the laundry basket. I'll brush my teeth before going to bed." When they get a hold on these goals, they learn a sense of self-direction, as well as a sense of accomplishment. The pursuit of these goals also provides a great opportunity for one-minute praisings.

The older kids get, the more challenging the goals can become, and the greater the successes and sense of accomplishment will be. But we start simple and easy when they're young and gradually build from there.

When my life is drawing to a close, I'm sure that any

money I've made or attention I've gained as a speaker or teacher or coach won't seem important. What will count then is walks I've taken with Bobbie, how I've related to my children, and whatever help I've been to others in their relationships. And you know, if I can keep my priorities straight, I'll realize that those are also the things that are important right now. How about you?

REFLECTIONS

1. Describe the ideal mother and the ideal father. Explain your response.

---

2. Willard Tate summarized parenting goals in five statements. Each statement is given below. Put each statement into your own words and give a brief, practical example of how you can use that concept.

  a. "We want to instill in our children the truth that God loves them unconditionally."

---

  b. "We want to teach them that God is for them."

---

  c. "God forgives, God forgives."

---

    d. *"We want our children to gain self-esteem by the way we dis-cipline."*

_____

_____

    e. *"We want our kids through our discipline to become self-dis-ciplined."*

_____

_____

    3. *What do you think the saying "Catch them doing something right" means?*

_____

_____

    4. *Give one example of how you can apply the concept of the One-Minute Parent.*

_____

_____

Chapter 12

Robbed by the Little Things

A proud tiger was walking through the jungle one day, roaring at every animal he met. "Who's the toughest animal in this jungle?" he growled. And they all answered, "You are, Mr. Tiger." He went through this scene with one animal after another.

Finally he walked up to an elephant and said with his usual bravado, "Who's the toughest animal in this jungle?" Whereupon the elephant wrapped his trunk around the tiger, picked him up, slapped him up against a tree three or four times, and finally let him fall down. The tiger looked up with his head spinning and said, "Look, just because you don't know the answer doesn't mean you have to get mad."

Unfortunately, life doesn't grab most of us like that and whack us in the head to wake us up. Instead, life has a way of rocking us to sleep. It's so easy to slip into ruts and let life go by without giving attention to the things that are really important. A rut, by the way, is just a grave with the ends knocked out. "Catch the little fox that ruins the vineyard," Solomon wrote. It's the little things, the subtleties of life, that do us in.

It's so tough to weigh the value of a day, of any one day in our lives. It's hard to see the importance of what we do or don't do today to build a relationship, to share some love, to get a job done. After all, there's always tomorrow. Besides that, we just don't see the connection between what we do today and what our lives will be ten or twenty years from now. So we get in the habit of saying, "What I do today isn't very important."

But every day matters, and every little thing we do or don't do matters. Many opportunities we'll have today to say a kind word or offer a helping hand or write an encouraging letter will never come our way again. Certainly this day will be gone forever once it's done.

Major Time on Minor Things

One of the keys to life, I'm convinced, is to spend major time on *major* things—not on *minor* things. To waste our precious minutes on things of little consequence is a tragedy.

"Major things must get major time."

I once asked the students in my college class, "What are the major things in life?"

"Well, relationships are major," one of them said.

"That's good," I said. "What else?"

"Getting a college degree. Keeping up good grades. Getting started in a career."

"Yes, those are all major. What else?"

"Starting a family."

"Uh huh. I'm still listening."

Finally one girl said, "Well, your spiritual life's major."

I thought that was a good answer, and I appreciated the honesty—they were really saying that our spiritual life is an afterthought. They weren't seeing it as major at all.

Sadly, they have a lot of company in that assessment in the Christian community. For many Christians, the only Bible teaching they expose themselves to is one sermon a week. That's twenty minutes, or maybe only ten or fifteen. How much can be said in a twenty-minute sermon? When I do seminars, I speak for six hours and still don't get in everything I'd like to say.

To go along with that brief sermon experience, the average Christian spends less than an hour a week reading his Bible. Yet he spends more than three hours a day, twenty-one hours a week, watching TV. It reminds me of the guy who said he thought he had half a mind to watch TV. I think he was right. Talk about spending major time on minor things!

Is it any wonder, then, that the typical Christian can't say who preached the Sermon on the Mount, can't name the four Gospels, and can't list even half the Ten Commandments? Subtleties, little things, letting one day after another slip away will take the Christian life away from us.

If you're a married man, think back to when you were courting your wife. How did you treat her? You used to bring her flowers, write her little notes, open car doors for her, give her a call if you were running late. Tell me, do you still do those affectionate things for her, or have you let the warmth slip away? If you're a woman, you can think of the little things that apply in your case.

Again, we can't weigh the consequences of neglecting our relationships with God or our spouse for one day; just one day doesn't seem to make a lot of difference. But I promise you that in twenty years, the consequences of all those individual days of being robbed by the little things will be only too clear.

The students in my classes today act and think a *little* different—not a lot. But wait until they keep thinking and doing as they are now for thirty years. There will be a vast difference in them. Life has a way of adding up the "little" things.

Asking the Wrong Questions

Sometimes when I talk about how little things, like too much TV, can rob our lives, I get the question from students—and sometimes from adults, too—"Well, what's wrong with it?" And that's often followed by, "Well, it doesn't really matter, does it? I don't let it affect me." But the problem is that those are the wrong questions to be asking, and any time you ask the wrong questions, you're going to get the wrong answers.

"Life has a way of adding up."

For example, a few years ago there was a tremendously popular book that posed the question, "Why do bad things happen to good people?" That's the wrong question to ask, so it wasn't surprising that the author didn't have many answers. The right question, in light of God's holiness and humanity's sin, is, "Why has God allowed so many to be happy and to live in such pleasure?"

The right question regarding something like TV is, "What's *right* with it?" Each of us has only so much time each day, and we've got to choose between the good and the best uses of it. Otherwise the subtleties of life will rock us to sleep and the minor things will devour major chunks of time.

Likewise with "It doesn't really matter, does it?" The right question is, "With what am I filling my mind?" because everything we come in contact with helps to shape us. We can never overestimate the power of influence, and TV is a powerful influence indeed. Everything matters.

Jim Rohn's writings have influenced my life very much. He tells this story: A little bird was crying, holding his wing over one eye. Another little bird said to him, "Why are you crying?"

The first bird pulled his wing back from over his eye.

"Oh, I see. The big bird has pecked out your eye. That's why you're crying."

"No, I'm not crying because the big bird pecked out my eye," the first bird said. "I'm crying because I let him."

One day, I believe, we'll either rejoice over what we did with our lives with God's help, or else we'll weep secretly over what we let life do to us. My prayer is that you and I will be among those who are able to rejoice in that day.

REFLECTIONS

"Many opportunities we'll have today to say a kind word or offer a helping hand or write an encouraging letter will never come our way again.
                                            Willard Tate

1. *Realizing that making something a priority means you will spend time, effort, and money on that priority, list the five key priorities in your life at this time.*

a. _____

b. _____

c. _____

d. _____

e. _____

2. *Read Matthew 6 carefully and consider the following questions:*

    a. *What is said about goals for the Christian?*

_____

_____

    b. *What is the cure for anxiety?*

_____

_____

    c. *How can we, as Christians, live in the real world and follow Matthew 6:31-34 to the letter?*

_____

_____

3. *Ecclesiastes 12:13, 14 sheds a great deal of light on our priorities. In your own words explain what Solomon is saying.*

_____

_____

Chapter 13

Drawing Near to the One Who Loves Us Best

Back in the early days of navigation, when ships were powered by the wind, sailors in Antarctic waters would sometimes see a frightening sight. As they were being blown one way, they'd see an iceberg coming toward them, cutting into the very teeth of the wind. They had no idea how that could be happening.

Eventually, of course, it was discovered that only a small fraction of the iceberg was visible above the waterline. Its huge, ponderous body was deep in an ocean current that bore it steadily along regardless of the surface tides or the winds of the moment.

It seems to me that all of us, man and woman, boy and girl, need to have our lives anchored deeply in something, too—something so deep and powerful that it moves us along our way on a predetermined course regardless of surface winds of circumstance or cash flow or whatever else happens from day to day. That something is a relationship with the One who loves us best, and we can learn how to establish that relationship through His Word.

Drawing Near

Earlier we discussed self image, or self worth. Think of this as a ladder, with the top rung being the limit to which you can accomplish. It's your self-made ceiling, your perceived potential. Now, picture yourself extending the ladder to accomplish more, to become a better gift to God, yourself and others. Regardless of how many rungs you add, the ladder will never reach to Heaven. To illustrate, suppose you attempt to swim to Hawaii. It matters little if you are a beginning swimmer or a world-class olympic record holder, you will still drown; it's of little consequence that you swam farther than I did—we both end up at the same place, drowned. We can't make it on our own.

We must establish and maintain an on-going, loving relationship with God through Jesus Christ. Jesus explains what a loving relationship is when He said, "If you love me, you will keep my commandments." So loving Jesus means following His word as found in His book.

If the impression is left that we automatically have a relationship with God simply because God loves us, it is a misunderstanding. God does love you, and will always love you; but God also demands that our hearts be in tune with His will. Knowing that God loves us is the most powerful thought that we humans can ever have. It provides the motivation to respond out of love.

There seem to be certain common qualities of heart of those who choose to draw near to God and receive His blessings.

First, an attitude and heart set on doing God's will. (Read I Ki. 8:17-19, II Chron. 30:15-20)

The second seems to be a willingness to submit to God's purpose. These people want God's will to be done more than they want their own will. Remember the prayer Jesus prayed in the garden prior to His death for our sins, "Not my will, but your will be done."

The third is a life of praise and thanksgiving. The

very existence of these people seems to be to praise God. They recognize where the blessings of life come from, and give God the glory and praise (Deut. 8:10-20). Remember the downward spiral we discussed (Rom. 1:21F) in chapter 7.

Once we have our hearts and attitudes right, are willing to submit to God, and desire to praise His name, we will have no resistance to keeping the commandments in His word.

God tells us that He takes a different view of the sins of these people. "He does not treat us as our sins deserve or repay us according to our iniquities" (Psa. 103:10). That's good news!

We all deserve to die, but, praise God, He has given His grace to those who draw near to Him (Lam. 3:22-24). Listen to the Holy Scripture: "Come near to God and He will come near to you" (James 4:8).

Praise God! We are treated special because we have a father-son relationship (Psa. 32:2).

The Seasons of Life

We need such a deep relationship with God because we all pass through seasons of life that try us and might otherwise destroy us. Winters, especially, are dark, hurting times when we really need to draw on God's love and strength. The fact that spring always follows winter offers some consolation, but by itself it's not enough. And in fairer weather, it's easy for the little things to rob us if our anchor doesn't go deep.

One of my deepest winters came when I was about sixteen and I changed from the religion of my father and grandfather to the church of which I'm now a part. That really hurt my father. In his point of view, I was saying I knew more than he did, and the effect was like slapping him in the face with a wet towel. Since he was hurting, he tried to hurt me in return, threatening things against me and himself.

I didn't handle it well, to say the least. It was a dark winter time. At one point I told my spiritual mentor that I didn't think I could take any more, but he said to me, "Just sit steady in the boat. Ride out the storm." Wise man that he was, he knew you just survive winter. You hang on and wait for the spring to come.

Sure enough, spring did finally come, and with it two great blessings—the opportunity to go to college, and my marriage to Bobbie, the most wonderful wife and mother in the world. (In the later years of his life, my father and I were also beautifully reconciled.)

We weathered other winters also—the Winters of financial struggle and hardship (which many are in even now)—but Spring always follows. Much of the fruit we enjoy in our lives now came out of those Springs.

Strengthening Our Relationship

How, then, do we strengthen our relationship with God? How do we "anchor" into a relationship with Him so that we can move steadily against the wind? I offer the things that have made the difference in my life in the hope that they'll do the same for you. I don't think there's any better way I could have brought this book to a close.

First, over time and with experience, we develop a trust in God that He really is going to see us through. I don't mean lip-service faith but a trust strong enough that we're willing to act on it.

"Trust is getting in the wheelbarrow."

Back in the days when such stunts were popular, there was a guy who one day stretched a tightrope over Niagara Falls. Then he got up on it and pushed a wheelbarrow over it all the way across the falls. By the time he turned around and came back, there was a large crowd watching him. "Tell me," he said, "do you think I can do that again?"

Yes, the people answered, we believe you have the ability.

Then he said, "But does anyone trust me enough to get in the wheelbarrow and go across with me?" The truly trusting person would have ended up in the wheelbarrow.

In Romans 8:28 we have this promise from God: "We know that all things work together for good to those who love God, to those who are the called according to His purpose." Do we really trust God to keep that pledge? Only with experience in finding Him faithful does that trust grow. We have to obey God. That's the real test. We put one foot in the wheelbarrow, then the other.

Next, we deepen the relationship as we stay close to His people in the church. Successful businesses have their people meet weekly or more for mutual encouragement and the sharing of wisdom. The church meets the same need spiritually.

Then we need to let someone love us. This means allowing people to get to know us, to get into our lives and really love us as we are. As we accept God's love for us through others, we'll grow closer to Him as well.

Naturally, we want to stay close to God in prayer and in His Word. I'm not going to try to dictate how much time this should involve, but an hour a week isn't enough.

Finally, we'll draw nearer to God as we reach out to help others. You see, the two parts of this book are closely connected. We get our love and sense of worth from God and then offer what we've found to others, and in giving of it, we find our own experience of it grows. So as the commercial says, we'll enjoy reaching out and touching someone. When we do, we'll find we're touching the Savior Himself.

REFLECTIONS

1. *What does Ephesians 3:14-20 tell us about our God?*

_____

_____

2. *How does the passage in Ephesians 3 relate to the "dark winters" of our lives to which the author referred?*

_____

_____

3. *Describe an incident in your life in which your faith in God saw you through.*

_____

_____

4. *Do you agree or disagree with the following statement? "Getting and keeping a close, personal relationship with God is our one and only goal as Christians." Explain your answer.*

_____

_____